Ty Alexander *from* **GORGEOUS IN GREY**

Things I Wish I Knew Before My Mom Died

Coping with Loss Every Day

Published by Mango Publishing Group, a division of Mango Media Inc.

Cover and Layout Design: Elina Diaz

Author Photo: Michael Williams

For permission requests, please contact the publisher at:

Mango Publishing Group
2850 Douglas Road, 3rd Floor
Coral Gables, FL 33134 USA
info@mango.bz

For special orders, quantity sales, course adoptions and corporate sales, please email the publisher at sales@mango.bz. For trade and wholesale sales, please contact Ingram Publisher Services at customer.service@ingramcontent.com or +1.800.509.4887.

Things I Wish I knew Before My Mom Died

Library of Congress Cataloging

ISBN: (paperback) 978-1-63353-388-2, (ebook) 978-1-63353-387-5

Library of Congress Control Number: has been applied for

BISAC category code: FAM014000 FAMILY & RELATIONSHIPS / Death, Grief, Bereavement

Printed in the United States of America

Dedication

This book is dedicated to all the daughters whose mothers were stolen by Heaven. We are now a part of a motherless tribe, and I will always fight for our sanity through my words and actions.

Table of Contents

Foreword

Ty has been in my professional orbit for about six years. I've always liked and respected her—and since this is a safe space, I'll admit to my girl crush (the hair!). But I should also admit that, in the past, I haven't been a huge self-help reader. I feel like no one has all the answers. ~~Except Michelle Obama.~~ Plus, I try to keep things simple. Life's terrifying, random and confusing, right? All you can do is absorb the punches with grace and embrace the goodness with gratitude. Outside of that, have ride-or-die girlfriends and one great vice (that doesn't hurt anybody). For me, donuts for dinner once a week keeps me sane. I balance this with carrot sticks so I feel like a responsible adult.

Ty's book isn't just self-help, though. It's a mix: a memoir, detailing her personal experience with the loss of her beloved mother and an inspirational guide on how to battle through. Ty's not telling you how to grieve. She's offering up her truth—and if a piece of it hits home for you, or gives you perspective, she's inviting you to take it and run. I remember when she was going through this. She was vocal about her mother's heartbreaking death on social media, and I remember being floored by her bravery. Ty didn't go around the grief. She went through it. And the loss was as intense, complicated, ecstatic, and emotionally fraught as her relationship with her mother was in life. Which makes sense. All mother/daughter relationships are complex—of course that energy would carry over, even after the loss. There's a comfort in knowing that, somehow.

Ty speaks of the relentless, shameless love of mothers. How mothers do whatever it takes to make their babies happy. Exhibit A: I'm writing this at 2 a.m. in a hotel bed next to my seven-year-old daughter, who's sleeping horizontally (as she does), with her feet shoved into the right side of my neck. I'm staying super-still so I don't wake her, because her insomnia is as bad as mine, and I want her to have a full night's sleep. I'll massage Icy Hot into my pummeled neck tomorrow morning, but who cares? Lina will wake up well-rested, happy—and blithely unaware that she physically abused her mother for eight hours.

When it comes to our mothers, we're all oblivious. We'll never know the everyday, banal sacrifices they made so we could blossom. A mother's secrets are oceans-deep. But we do know that mothers are our entry into the world, the reason we're here—so when they go, who are we? My entire self-image as a woman was cultivated as a reaction to my mother's. When she's gone, how will I identify myself? I can't imagine the answer. I haven't experienced this loss, and there's nothing that can prepare me for it. I can only hope that I can move through it with as much dignity and honesty as Ty.

Thank you for opening up and sharing your story with us.

—*Tia Williams*
author of *The Perfect Find*

Introduction

F or the past eight months, I've been staring at my laptop while actively thumping the letters on my keyboard attempting to complete some kind of sentences (read: I've been pretending to write this book). From the moment I was approached to write a book, I managed to talk myself out of all the reasons why I should write a book. Writing a book is really the most logical step for me since I do consider myself a pretty accomplished blogger (not so humble brag). I've been doing this for six years. I've managed to cultivate my little space on the Internet into enough income to pay for the overpriced box me and my boyfriend rent to live in New York. I've even got a few contributors for my blog so that I can take advantage of those last minute flight deals to travel whenever I feel like it. My creative director friend will tell anyone that I am one of the best copywriters she's worked with, and yet still I feel like a fraud. I have developed a serious case of impostor syndrome. My daily writing routine involved typing a few paragraphs and then deleting them all. I'd do that for about four or five hours. Then I'd wake up the next day and start that process all over. I kept asking myself, "Why am I even writing this book?" And I'm for certain that some of you will ask: what makes her such an expert?

Am I an expert?

Well, here's my story. My mother was diagnosed with stage 4 lymphoma and died within that same year. I found myself aggressively riding on the horns of depression. And I promise you, that ride was an epic fail wrapped in some sort of poisonous chemical that likely resembled arsenic. Somewhere along this journey, I acquired extra bodyweight equal to the size of a baby panda—except I was not nearly as cute. I didn't sleep. I was really close friends with 3 a.m. I couldn't let a day pass without waiting up for her. I was moderately attached to my bed, at least until 2 in the afternoon. When you are grieving, no one tells you that there isn't a magical yellow brick road that you can follow to return to your normal life. No one tells you that your normal life is gone.

Because what was normal to me was gone, depression kicked in.

To me, depression seemed like a trivial experience, a defect of human nature. Being depressed just never made any sense to me. It's feeling everything but yet feeling nothing at all. And I didn't understand why you couldn't just ignore or get over all those contradictory feelings. That is until depression happened to me. Depression feels like being stuck on a huge ship all by yourself. And that ship has been parked in the middle of an ocean for what feels like months, maybe even years. And that ocean is filled with self-pity, anxiety, misery, fear and then sprinkled with a little self-doubt for added effect. Everything about depression is inconvenient for you and for me. That's what depression feels like.

From the moment my mother realized she'd rather die than fight cancer, I decided I would document every emotion I had because... I'm a writer. That's what we do. Plus, my mother and I were so close. I was her Blue Ivy; she was my Beyoncé. I didn't know what else to do but to write. I didn't realize that I was secretly planting the seeds I needed for this book. Now I have notes scribbled everywhere and on everything. Millions of drafts are saved in my Evernote app. Post-Its are strategically placed all over my desk, the fridge and on the mirror in my bathroom. There are bits and pieces of my experiences in different journals all over my room (because the same journal was never available when my thoughts arrived). My thoughts are even left on semi-dirty napkins stuffed in those random notebooks. Excuse me while I make sense of my thoughts for this book.

But despite all that I have been through, despite that ship in the middle of the ocean I had been chilling on, it's becoming clear to me that my mother's death was not entirely damaging to my existence. At some point, I stopped being mad at cancer, my dysfunctional kinfolks and myself and realized that her death had become a series of life-enhancing lessons and gifts. Life had served me the biggest bittersweet cupcake it could find.

This book represents 153 pages of life revelations that I would not have ever known existed without losing my mother. And that fucking sucks. It sucks that I had to sacrifice so much to learn these lessons. It sucks that it took me so long to get here. And to be perfectly honest with you, I'm not even sure where *here* is. I just know that *here* is better than that ship that was parked in the middle of an ocean, for what felt like months, that was filled with self-pity, anxiety, misery, fear and then sprinkled with a little self-doubt for added effect. So to answer my own question— and maybe yours—that's why I decided to write this book. I don't claim to be the expert on grief but I'm an expert at my own grieving. Hopefully, you can learn something about yours from reading about mine.

Even though I don't know you personally, I don't ever want you to feel guilty about leaving the state you grew up in to pursue your dreams while your parent wilts away from cancer. Oh wait sorry, that's my guilt, not yours.

The point is, after reading my book I just want you to feel the gratitude that I do now. I hope that my book teaches you to be a bit more patient with your grief. I'm hoping that my words, my truth, will grant you that mustard seed of faith you need to survive your own grieving process. And because I know grief may have hijacked your heart and soul, I hope that you allow my book to teach you how to love again. I hope my book inspires you to live again. And most importantly, I want my book to give you the permission you need to love and forgive yourself for everything you did or didn't do.

Because Heaven stole our moms, you and me, we're a part of this motherless tribe. So I want you to stand tall in your truth and live far beyond your fears. That's what I'm doing.

Chapter

01

We've been duped; everyone dies!

{ Why you should shamelessly love hard }

When I was a kid, my parents welcomed and entertained me and my brother's every wish. And I mean, every wish! It's the main reason my brother and I don't really know each other (apart from our six year age difference). We were never forced to play together. I had my things, and he had his. Gosh, I miss those days. I still envy the closet I owned as a kid. My mother spoiled the shit outta us, and I was her precious little baby girl. I had an endless supply of Barbies and Cabbage Patch Kids. I had every electronic gadget you could think of: VCR. Boombox. Cassette player. Record player. TV. I had them all as soon as they were released. When I wasn't "jamming on the one" (remember that episode of *The Cosby Show*?) pretending to be Whitney Houston, I was teaching Barbie and her friends how to host the best darn party ever in her three-story dream house with the Corvette parked out front. My therapist later analyzed the early years of my life. We determined that the cause was probably my parents' guilt over my dad being absent reimagined as love (but that's another book).

By the time I was in high school, we were the definition of spoiled middle-class kids. Thankful, but spoiled.

I had masterfully managed to try tap dance, ballet, piano lessons, saxophone lessons...you name it, I tried it. Unfortunately, because I often quit, I was mediocre, at best, at all of them. But my mom let me try anything I wanted to do. Any and every dream I had was honored, mostly without question. So when I had this bright idea that we should get a family pet, we got a family pet. My parents got a parakeet, thinking it would be easier than getting a puppy. Ha! Wait. Actually, I can't remember if that was my idea or my mom's. But, in my mind, I had all of these plans to love my new pet and to teach my bird how to talk back to me. We'd be besties for life.

I'd watched *The Flintstones* reruns faithfully after school. So when my mom asked what I was going to name the bird, I knew I wanted her to be "Pebbles." Pebbles was a tiny little thing but she was gorgeous. She was this bright canary yellow and ocean blue color and had soft silky wings. I loved that damn bird. Pebbles was the first thing you saw when you came into our house. I'd come home from school each day and maybe spend an hour or two trying to teach her to talk back to me. You should also know that I gave up on my lessons with Pebbles after about a week. Playing with Barbie and her friends proved to be a much easier task. Plus, someone had to drive Barbie's new ride and help her host her last minute soirees. I swear I tried my best to take care of Pebbles. And I thought I was doing a good job. You know, as good as any child takes care of any one thing. I hadn't had that bird for more than a month when I came home from dance class and noticed that Pebbles was gone. Her cage was gone. I instantly went into a full-on kiddie panic attack when I saw that her little area in our living room was replaced with a brand new wooden coffee table with a pretty piece of stained glass in the middle of it. The nasty stench Pebbles caused (that really bothered me and my mom) was also gone, swapped out for my mom's favorite household scent: Pine-Sol. When I finally stopped bubble-snot crying, I asked my mom what happened. She told me that Pebbles had flown away. My mom had this way of answering certain questions so abruptly and firmly that you didn't dare ask her to elaborate.

I was devastated and kiddie depressed (read: when children refuse to eat and sit in the corner voluntarily and pout). I was mad as hell. For weeks, I was really shook up over this damn bird. But more than any of those emotions I felt, I knew I had let Pebbles down. I told my mother I was quittin' school. I know that's a laughable demand, but I felt that school was the reason I didn't take better care of Pebbles; that she would have never left if I were home more. My mom knew how dramatic her child could be, so my request to quit school was arrogantly dismissed like those nasty ass black jellybeans during Easter.

After that, we never ever got another pet. My mom was over it, and she become voluntarily oblivious to every single request I made for a puppy…or a fish!

I think I was in my twenties when my mom slipped up and told the real story behind Pebbles's disappearance. Get this: my bird didn't really run away. I bet you guessed that though?! My mom let her lighthearted confession casually slip out over Thanksgiving dinner while we all devoured her infamous homemade crab cakes. She said she woke up one morning and that "damn bird" was just dead. (Here's where you can insert a lot of hearty laughter and a few deep sighs of relief from my aunts and my older cousins. As if they all knew!) She said: "Pebble's was a bad idea anyways. I knew you weren't gonna take care of dat bird!" So when she found Pebbles' lifeless body, she cleaned all traces of her existence and then threw her out into our back yard for the stray dogs and the field mice to have their way (the dramatic kid in me still oozes out sometimes).

I ain't gonna lie, I was mad as fuck when my mom told me that. I quickly changed the subject so that I wouldn't embarrass myself by yelling at mom for lying to me. Looking back, the adult in me knows that she was just trying to protect me and my little thug tears (read: those uncontrollable tears followed by snot and hiccups). She didn't want me to experience death, even if the loss was just "dat bird." So she unapologetically lied straight to my face to keep me safe from my feelings.

As a mother, I get it. You wanna hold your children's tiny little fragile feelings close because you know that they are breakable. And it sucks when shit breaks. But I do wish my mom had been upfront with me. The reality of it was that I was going to have a mini panic attack and be kiddie depressed anyways because Pebbles was gone. You can't fix that. It happened. And in the grand scheme of reality checks—I hate to break this to you—everyone dies. That's right, we've all been duped, people! It's one of the few guarantees in this thing we call life. Everyone and every thing dies. Everyone and every thing has a beginning and an end, a start and a finish. Abruptly or semi-planned, it's gonna happen, my beloveds.

> **"**
> *Everyone and every thing has a beginning and an end...*
> **"**

I know, all of this is *mad* depressing. It's that unchanging truth we all ignore to our own demise. Then we spend hours, days, months, years, decades and even lifetimes grieving instead of actually living and loving.

If we all shamelessly loved each other, then death would be an easier pill to swallow. If we loved without regret, without guilt, without judgment—you know: shamelessly—then death would just be the price we paid for a love so grand.

Can you imagine a love so relentless, so shameless, that you'd never want that person to be anything but happy and overjoyed? Even if it meant that death had to happen. It's the kinda love that allows your mom to drop all of her dreams, allowing you to experience your own. It's a love so monumental that it lasts beyond your last breath in this world. That's shameless love! It wasn't until I didn't have my mom's love present every day that I realized it was so shameless. She always protected me, and my little thug tears, at any cost.

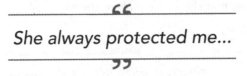

She always protected me...

I was twenty years old when I left home. I had just had a baby. I wanted to come and go as I pleased. My mom and I had gotten into a huge argument about the usual nothings that life brings any young adult. Freshly graduated from the world of teenagedom, I was fittin' to flex my new adulthood because…it was mine and it was new! With my one-year-old son on my hip, I told my mom where she could go and how she could get there. Gasp! I knew she wouldn't physically try to kill me as long as I had my son in my arms. I planned on never coming back to that house again. Because she was right. If I didn't wanna play by my parents' rules, then I should just leave. Just before I stormed out of the kitchen and attempted to slam *her* front door, she grabbed the doorknob with one hand and caught my wrist with the other and said, "You can leave my house if you want to, but remember you can *always* come back home!"

There were a lot of times when I was in the dark, without electricity, holding my son and wishing to be back home. I was fired from jobs more times than I care to remember (or admit), but my pride never let me go back home. Instead, I'd visit often to grab up my share of parental guidance, soap opera talk, and *duh*…those infamous, homemade crab cakes that she loved making for me.

> ❝
> *...her love was so shameless that she didn't care...*
> ❞

When I was thinking of how to explain shameless love to you, I thought back to that day I left. Because something happened to me that day. Because her love was so shameless that she didn't care who judged her for my actions. Her love never changed, no matter what I did or what I said. My mom's love liberated me! It liberated me to be something more than I ever could have imagined. And, of course, despite that liberation she bestowed upon me, I managed to turn my 20s into one long ass theatrical episode of *Punk'd* and then spent my 30s cleaning up that masterpiece of foolery. But her shameless love gave me permission to think beyond the moments that made me weak. It's what has made me strong. That shameless love gave me permission to believe that I could be great. That shameless love gave me permission to stand strong in what she taught me to be right or wrong. That shameless love gave me permission to make absurd mistakes that led to phenomenal lessons. Like this book!

{ The grenade life threw at me: Goodbye, Mom }

And then, life fucking happened! There was this global sized grenade thrown down at my feet. I didn't run. I couldn't run. I think the worst part of death is that you can't run from it. And now, there was no one to cover up my wounds before they began. I was forced to face death once again. But this time by myself.

My mom's obituary reads, "Yolanda "Denny" D. Brown passed away peacefully at home surrounded by her family on Sunday, April 28, 2013." I always have to check the obituary for the exact date because I've managed to purposely discard that day's existence. It's not like a memory to me; it's my reality. And even though I don't remember the day, it's a reality that I replay repeatedly like a sappy ass movie, over and over and over again. It's kinda like each time I watch *The Notebook*. I get all sucked into the storyline of how they fell in love. Then I swoon over their love and hope for its continuation, as if I don't know the ending. Like I don't know that they peacefully die, holding hands together, but dead nonetheless. It's like I don't know that I've been duped and everyone dies. Including moms. Including my mom.

When my mom died, my family treated me like that 10-year-old little girl whose parakeet had just died. Everyone was semi-lying to me for the sake of saving me from my thug tears and kiddie depression spells. My entire family tiptoed around my feelings. My Aunt Katy called me on the Wednesday before my mom died. I was wrapping up at work when I picked up my phone to say hello. There was this long, uncomfortable pause. It was the kind of pause that was too long for anything good to happen next. You know what kinda pause I'm talkin' bout. It's the kinda pause that gives up the tape for what's about to come next. It's the bad news kinda pause. That agonizing, heart shattering, unthinkable bad news! She told me that the hospice nurse had been by my parents' house to examine my mom, and "it's not looking good."

I. Almost. Snapped.

Like, legit straight-jacket, mental-facility-worthy type of snapping. I mean let's be real here, people. It ain't been looking good since that day Mommy went to the hospital and the doctor said, "Can you excuse us, I need to talk to your mother in private?" There was a similar uncomfortable pause that day, too.

I pulled a Kanye and let Aunt Katy finish because she's my favorite, and I know she means well all the time! She said, "You should come home now, they're giving her just a few days." I calmly, almost without any feeling in my voice, said, "Ok."

OK? What. The. Fuck!

My entire body slowly crept down into my desk chair, and I was basically sprawled out on the floor. I could feel my bottom lip trembling, but the thug tears that I had been prepping myself for since the moment my mom went home with hospice just wouldn't come out. Instead, my skin got hot. Then it got cold. I thought I was going to faint. I dropped my cell phone, and on my hands and knees I turned to my co-worker and whispered, "My mother. Is dying."

My mom was supposed to live forever...

It was the first time I said it out loud. It was the first time that I believed that death could actually happen to my mom. It was the first time that I believed that I had been duped. She was supposed to beat cancer and live to see my *every thing* happen gloriously. She was supposed to be there for my wedding, my grandchildren (although I don't ever want any), my first house, my first book. My mom was supposed to live forever, even though I had just spent the past eight months joking with her about what the Upper Room would look like when she got there. We had so many questions. Like: do you have to wait in line to see Jesus? Because I feel like Jesus is really popular in Heaven, so it might take her a minute to get settled. Is there a meeting that happens between Jesus and all the new angels? Then I wondered: do you see Jesus first and then God? Or does anyone really see God? Listen! I had (and still have) so many questions. But this is what we talked about. We knew that death was happening. But when it happened...

That hour-long train ride from my Midtown job to my little box that I called home in Brooklyn was absolutely miserable. I was on a crowded subway train watching people watch me watch them while I violently bubble-snot cried. I didn't even have the energy to wipe the tears off, so I was just wet as fuck from my eyeballs to my chest. Literally! The front of my sheer white work blouse was soaked and showed my fellow passengers more than any woman wanted to show a crowded New York train.

{ How I dealt with my mother's death }

Then something happened. I heard a song that triggered what I believe was my revelation. I realized that my mom would always be with me no matter what. Here's why this is really a sign from Baby Jesus: The song that I credit as my revelation is a song I don't even remember adding to any of my playlists on Spotify. Ever. It's a song that I probably would have skipped on any other train ride, but that day I let "Lovely Day"—the Jill Scott version—be great inside my headphones. I immediately stopped crying. I turned my volume up as loud as it could go and then stuffed my earbuds a little further in my ears. Jill started to hum. The beat dropped. The bass got louder. The supply of water for my tears paused as if a barricade had just appeared before them. My mind was an eerie kind of calm.

Now, the song pops up in my playlist whenever I need it. Whenever I need to feel my mom and be reminded of the love we share. And I still get chills when I hear it. My little baby-thug tears appear. I always think back to that moment when my mother became my personal angel. I've always believed it's the moment she got her wings.

Last year, me and my best friend went to Oprah's *The Life You Want Weekend*. Our one and only goal was to be in the building with Mama O. And maybe we wanted to be inspired. We got there super early. The kinda early that allows for hundreds of selfies in an empty stadium. We had decent seats, and we made sure we came with an open heart and nonjudgmental ears. At the time I was desperately seeking some inspiration, some stimulation, some something. I needed to be awakened. I was writing for an online publication that indisputably made the inside of my soul crawl to nothingness and burn a slow death, repeatedly, daily. I felt like my relationship with my boyfriend was crumbling (truth is, it was). And since my mom died, I hadn't spoken to or had a real conversation with my dad outside of a few birthday and happy father's day texts. Life for me had become an extreme chore, and I was just going through the motions. I was hoping and praying that Oprah could offer up some free therapy because I was also broke.

Please believe me when I tell you that Oprah and her clan preached the good word of "get your life together" all weekend long. That weekend really dug deep into my soul and deposited much-needed life affirmations and universal testimonies that I needed to hear to keep going. When it was all over, Oprah made her closing remarks. I could barely concentrate on her message. I was so in my feelings. And anyone who knows me knows that I really hate feeling feelings. But while Oprah was speaking, I was regretting the fact that my mom and I never really experienced things like this together. At best, we'd watch T.D. Jakes preach that good word on Sundays during our Bedside Baptist worshipping. My mom hated planes and tried her best to *not* travel too far outside of that little Maryland town we were from. I just kept thinking about how much my mom would have loved to be there to witness Oprah and friends. My mom and I never got a chance to do any of the really cool stuff I was being afforded since I was a now this popular blogger/writer.

We wanted to beat the crowd, so we started to make our way to the steps just as Oprah was wrapping up her speech. If you're into melodramatic, clichéd story endings then you might have already guessed what happened as Oprah went to exit stage left. OMG, yes "Lovely Day" by Jill Scott played in the background as Oprah ended the evening. You can absolutely cue your own personal thug tears right now because I almost laid completely out on the floor when Jill started to hum. When that beat dropped. When the bass got louder. But instead of making a complete fool out of my best friend (because frankly I never cared that much if I made a fool out of myself), I chose to close my eyes and allow my mom's presence to settle comfortably in my heart and in my mind. Before that moment I was so distraught. I was searching for something in the world to kick me in the chest and beg me to start living again. And at that moment, I did. It became an unthinkable point in my life. Suddenly, my life had purpose again. My mom's death had purpose again. That singular moment changed how I felt about her death. It changed how i thought about death as a whole.

In the beginning of my grief, I completely ignored it. I never used past tense when I spoke of my mom. I remember having a panic attack when my dad asked me to come to their house and clean out my mom's closet. I was livid. She hadn't even been dead a week and he wanted me to throw all of our memories away. Like they meant nothing to us, to him! I couldn't understand why he wanted her things gone so soon. If I had it my way (and, of course, I did) I'd keep everything the same. I wanted everything to still feel and smell like my mom. I wanted to be able to open her bathroom door and smell Elizabeth Arden's Red Door perfume. I wanted the smell to be so disrespectful it smacked you on the top of the nose when you entered her room. It really didn't matter if she was no longer physically there with me, with us. Yes, in my mind, I knew she was gone. But I figured that if everything in my parents' house still left traces of my mom, then it would *maybe* feel like death never happened. Like she never left us for her rightful place in the Upper Room. It would feel like she never died.

> ❝
> ## I could feel that she wasn't afraid of death...
> ❞

But she did die. And I couldn't ignore that. After watching her fight cancer for almost a year, I learned that the last stages of her fight awakened this feeling of inevitability about death. And I think that must have been liberating to my mom. I could feel that she wasn't afraid of death anymore. She was really ready to die. That's how we ended up in a conversation about what people do in Heaven. She didn't have to manage her fear about death anymore. It was weird, but she had begun to include her death as a part of her experience. She started to believe that if she could prepare for her death, then she'd crush the power that death had over her. And after pouting and releasing a few thug tears (there's a theme here, guys) I realized that's how I had to deal with her death. Because we've all been duped. Everyone dies!

So I started to live with intention. I promise you that this is something that I work on daily. It doesn't come naturally to me. I don't think it's natural for anyone. Sometimes I need Jill Scott *and* Oprah to remind me that I have a purpose, and I have to find an intent to live. Having intent in your life is something that, just when you think that you've mastered it, you completely forget about it. You go back to pouting and having kiddie panic attacks. The reality of losing the biggest love of my life is the hardest to accept. The rush of feelings I have at the sound of the word "mom," the anxieties, the sleepless nights, the heartache of never hearing her voice again has all brought me to my knees. But my intent is not to live a happy life without my mom. I understand now that processing my grief doesn't mean that there will ever be any less emotional distress for me. It just means that it is possible, through my struggle, to come out on top. I've learned that my intent to live a happy life involves constantly figuring out how to be forever surrounded by her undying love.

And I don't know if that's the right way or the wrong way, but that's how I deal with death!

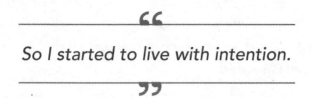

So I started to live with intention.

Things To Repeat To Yourself

Toast to the loves of your life...

...the ones that inspire a special type of love that completely liberates

your soul.

Let knowing that we've all been duped...

...steer your vision of life.

Change what death means and feels like to you.

Embrace your thug tears.

Let them out to play whenever they want.

They can keep you sane.

Chapter

02

When
fragmented
families
grieve

{ The fruits of my poisoned family tree. }

When I first decided to write this book, I deeply contemplated a whole lot of things. From if I would even be qualified to write a book, to what to include or exclude from it. You can imagine what kind of anxiety and doubt writing a memoir/self-help mashup brings about. One of the things I went back and forth with was whether or not I should let y'all in on one of my most treasured dirty little secrets—my dysfunctional ass family. I feel like we all come from one, right? And since this book is all about grieving and what I've learned along the way, I felt I'd be remiss if I didn't share the parts of me that aren't so pleasant and charming. The parts that I am ashamed of. The skeletons I've been keeping in my closet. I had to tell the tough stories that also show the parts of me that were shaped without my consent. In order to truly know who I am as a person, as a writer and also as someone who is grieving, I felt like you had to understand where I came from. I had to unravel how I got to this place of sheer contentment. Basically, the how and the why I don't have any fucks to give.

But I also needed to be fair to my family. Did I really want to put my family "on blast" like this? A lot of what I remember as a child was built on painful secrets that, by virtue of an unspoken code we all know as "family loyalty," I was never able to share or talk about. And because of that asinine code, a part of me felt responsible for holding those secrets tight and out of your reach.

I've changed my mind.

At her funeral, a few of our family members told these heartwarming stories about my mom, some of which I had never even heard before. It was stories of them together. It was their memories together. Afterward, we all headed to the church basement for a few funeral favorites...greasy fried chicken, overcooked green beans, and watered down coleslaw. When we returned to the house, I was left sitting on the floor in the middle of my parents' empty living room by myself. Everyone had left. Even my dad went to party his grief away. I was in an empty home with just old pictures of my mom and the smell of her hospital sheets. I was left alone with my thoughts and with this new annoyance called grief. I haven't spoken to much of my mom's side of my family since that day they left me. That was three years ago! My dad sometimes calls on birthdays and holidays. Some of my cousins will leave me "I miss your face" or "You're doing so well" types of messages on my Facebook page. But when the grieving started for all of us, it felt like I was forgotten.

Most of my family on my mom's side went completely Casper the Friendly Ghost on me. I used "friendly" to describe my family disconnect because it doesn't feel like it's blatant or intentional.

...my life felt like normal family foolery.

I can't remember saying or doing anything that would make them never want to talk to me again (I don't think?). I never got the phone calls or the Facebook messages about our gatherings with authentic Maryland steamed crabs and white potato pies, so at first their absence in my life felt like normal family foolery.

For me, my family was always just me, mom, dad and my brother. Because, when it came to my mom's side of the family, we were kinda the "black sheep" as the saying goes. It sucks because I'm not entirely sure why we were the black sheep. I just know that my mom wasn't raised by my grandmother, and things got tricky when my grandmother had another child after my mom. There's lots of resentment and anger that I'll never fully understand because, well, my mom is dead and I've never asked for the full story. But I know that it affected us all.

Outside of my black sheep inheritance, I was the lil' cute-but-bratty girl who thought she knew everything and rolled her eyes a little too hard at the adults whenever she was asked to do something she didn't want to do. And I always managed to get caught, too. I was one of those self-indulged grandkids who always bailed when it was family day at grandma's church. It was mom's fault, she said I didn't have to go if I didn't want to. So I didn't. I was also the one who left the small town that birthed me in search of something more and didn't look back. So since I was the black sheep, I didn't expect the support of my family outside of my parents and my brother. Until I saw what support really was and what it felt like.

I had found this new support by way of the World Wide Web, and that support unabashedly stood up for me when I was in my darkest days of grief. It felt fucking fantastic. When I couldn't get out of bed and I'd post cryptic social media messages, my Twitter followers knew. My Instagram followers knew. My Facebook followers knew. They'd send me messages over and over again until I responded to them saying that I was ok. And even after those messages, they'd message me again in a few days just to be sure that I wasn't lying to them. I thought about all the times my family called to check on me after my mom died.

Zero! It was zero freaking times. Not once had any of my family on my mom's side called to check on me and my grief. Then I got mad. Like really mad. Like, *big* mad!

"

...maybe my healing will also help you...

"

So now I really don't have two fucks to give about how they'll feel reading this part of my book because, frankly, I don't think they will even support me and read my book. I also feel certain that this confession is a part of my healing. And maybe my healing will also help you uncover your truth in grieving. I can't ignore that. I won't ignore that. You are more important to me. Hell, I am more important to me.

"A dysfunctional family is any family with more than one person in It."

—Mary Karr, author of The Liars' Club

Like some of you, I was raised in a traditional blue-collar household. I was fortunate enough to have two working parents who I always thought were happily married. I have one brother that I begged for but secretly wished that the baby delivery people would come back and get. He just took too long to get there (read: we are six years a part), and I had already gotten used to being the only child.

Our backyard and bedrooms were big enough that we were never forced to communicate and be real siblings who liked each other. That was my family.

_____ **"** _____

I knew that my family was falling apart.

_____ **"** _____

Our public lives promoted normalcy with a universal code language of, "We're all doing just fine. We are just fine." The biggest lie ever told to everyone! You know that appearances can be deceiving, and ours was just that. Behind closed doors, I knew that my family was falling apart. It had fallen apart. It wasn't until I became an adult who was having adult experiences that I realized we all grow up with some level of family chaos and unpredictability. I'd argue that this is normal family interaction simply because we all carry old wounds and baggage from our youth. Our pride and the respect for our families will never allow us to admit that. But I promise you it's true. You know what else is true? The children who have to live inside of that family chaos and unpredictability will become deficient in a lot of ways. After my teeny-tiny stint in therapy, I realized why I didn't trust the majority of people who claimed to love me (with the exception of my mom, of course). Growing up, it felt like everyone around me claimed to love me, but they were all lying. They were all liars. I never knew who I was supposed to believe. I would see something happen, or be involved in what I believed to be a pure catastrophe, and I'd be forced to lie about it. Soon I believed those lies. I believed I was doing the right thing by lying to everyone about our lives. That is the fruit of my poisoned family tree.

{ Uncovering and admitting dysfunction }

Most of the world envisions alcoholics and drug addicts as homeless bums who have been abandoned by life and annoyingly reside on our streets. Some of us view addicts as the men and women of our world who have royally betrayed their God-given talents for a cheap plastic bottle of vodka wrapped in a brown paper bag or a dirty needle filled with life's so-called greatest high. Google any statistic about addiction, and you will read that we're all wrong. Few addicts fit this visual we've conjured up. Most addicts are functional. My family addicts were or, should I say, are. I'll never know what life moments actually led my dad to use drugs. I've always wondered: what was the evolution of addiction? I can imagine that the anxiety and pressure that comes with marrying your pregnant high school sweetheart could have been overwhelming. Or maybe it was just as simple as a case of casual drug use gone insanely wrong. Or did he start with a lil' Mary Jane and then life became this unbelievable unicorn of a monster that he could no longer ride solo, so he invited hardcore drugs to join him on the journey? What was it? Who knows? Do I even care? I've never even asked my dad for his truth. And in real life, I probably won't. I'm not sure that his truth matters much when I think of my journey and what it means. But it is our biggest family secret—that I know of—and I'm pretty sure I just violated family code by telling you.

Oh well!

But this part of my world was crucial to dissect in order to understand my grieving process. As a child, I consciously denied my feelings about my dad's addiction. So when my mom died, I found myself immediately denying those feelings a place in my soul. I'm pretty sure this is why I hate feeling feelings.

I remember it was father-daughter week at my school. My dad missed every single activity. It sucked. I was bummed out. My friends began to ask where my dad was. I lied. I said that he was shipped off for duty in the Gulf War. War people! And I repeated it so much that I started to believe that shit. But the truth was his job sent him to get sober at this rehabilitation center a few hours from our house. Ultimately, to get better for his family, for us. But it was embarrassing to me. He had been away for a while before we visited him. So I had gotten really bitter about all the things he had missed and the fact that I had to lie about where he was. I felt like couldn't tell my friends the truth. It's hard to explain, but even as a kid I knew that his truth was our secret to keep. "My dad's an addict" isn't really a great conversation starter as a kid. I was ashamed, and it's just not something I felt like I could share. It felt like family business. Shit, I still feel like deleting this whole chapter.

Despite my embarrassment, my mom eventually convinced me to go and visit my dad. We went maybe one or two times (per my really vague childhood memories that I may have blocked out of my mind). I remember that he was staying in this really big fancy, lavish house. And there were a lot celebrities there with him, too. Some of the patients there I had even seen on the soap operas that me and my mom watched. My dad had gotten to be really close friends with one of the guys there. He was a former wrestler. Boy, did I love wrestling! I watched it every week and could tell you all the superstar wrestlers and their signature moves. My dad got him to sign my gym bag. Meh. I thought it was really cool to have at first. But I was still ashamed of my dad and that dumb ass gym bag, so I threw it in the trash and continued to lie to my friends. I had managed to build this denial system purely out of a logical and sensible purpose. There was this sense of shame and embarrassment that I don't think I ever got rid of. But as a kid, denial was what I needed to do to survive. I hadn't learned how to process any of these big, adult feelings I was having for this big, adult moment I was experiencing. And I truly believe that if I hadn't created that system for that experience, then I would be in a different place psychologically.

> 66
> ## *...pretended that grief was not happening.*
> 99

When grief first showed up in my world that's how I tried to treat it: with my denial system. I unconsciously pretended that grief was not happening. I bounced back like it was just a thing that happens. In the grand scheme of things, at the very core of what death is, it's just this *thing* that happens to us all at some point in our lives. Like I said, we've been duped; everyone dies. The end happens to everyone and everything. But when I tried to, let's say, self-medicate my grief, all those years of refining my denial got in my way. As a child, it was normal to skip and jump around my feelings. Now as an adult, it was a draining and toxic experience for me.

"If you don't take the time to work on the life you want, you're eventually going to be forced to spend A LOT of time dealing with the life you DON'T want."

—*Kevin Ngo, author of* Let's Do This! 100 Powerful Messages to Help You Take Action

Even though my dad had been sober for years, it was time
that I truly uncovered and admitted my dysfunction.

My father's addiction was just the surface of my problems.
Maybe that's my next book (or a year-long therapy bill).
But I realized that the longer I denied my dysfunction,
the worse I felt. I become more depressed. I had to learn
how to become independent of other people and my past
experiences. There was this interdependency that ruled
my life. Even though I was a grown up and I had a child of
my own who very much needed me to be his mother. Even
though I lived on my own for over a decade in a different
city than my parents. Even though I had a job that paid my
bills most of the time. Even though I was adulting, I always
knew that my parents, my mom to be specific, would be
there to bail me out of any problem that I had. When
my mom died, my dependency abruptly ended and the
detachment process began.

{ Honoring detachment as a life lesson }

That life support my mom gave me for some 30-odd
years was immediately unplugged when she died. I was
no longer the same person. I had no clue who I was.
I spent the first year of my grief trying to analyze and
basically control every single moment of my life. I think
it's what we all do when the void of detachment hits us.
We unconsciously do anything to make ourselves feel

complete again. I was so lost without my mom. So I started to aggressively pacify my detachment with non-stop movement. I mean I was busy. I overbooked every minute of the day. As a result, I barely remember what 2013 looked or felt like. I am still surprised that I survived that first year without my mom. From the minute my mom took her last breath that April, I checked all the way the fuck out of my feelings. I ain't wanna feel nothing! And I didn't at first.

We buried my mom on a Saturday, and the Saturday after that I was turning up with my blogger friends at a Rihanna concert at the Barclays Center in Brooklyn. Our concert experience was sponsored by a hair brand, so the food and libations were in abundance. I ate and drank everything that passed by me and even some things on other people's plates. I remember people regularly asking me if I was ok, like all night. Duh, I'm here so yeah I am ok. That was a lie, and I was starting to get annoyed. They were making me remember why I wasn't fucking ok. But this was the only way I knew how to survive my grief.

When I wasn't traveling or at events in the city, I would stay at my job until a crude and ungodly hour. It would be almost ten or eleven o'clock in the evening, and I would still be tapping on my keyboard writing stories for the week for both my blog and my full-time editor gig. I'd even go into the office on the weekends. I'd just sit at work all day

watching TV and writing. I knew that after 10 p.m. the
trains heading back to Brooklyn would be operating at their
typical snail's pace. When I finally got home, I'd just want
to go to sleep. When I was on the train, I'd concentrate on
learning the words to every song that played (to know me
is to know that I never know the words to songs). If I kept
my mind occupied every single second possible, there'd be
no missing her, no thinking about how difficult my life was
because I'd be too tired to think about it. The goal was to
zone all the way out and enter this world that I had created
for myself where feelings were absolutely forbidden. I gave
myself up as a tribute for my feelings. But in 2014, the
first deathiversary arrived and I woke up to all the emotions
I was hoarding from the year before. Except now they were
suffocating the shit outta me.

I did what I thought I could never do. I felt. I sat down one
weekend and I felt all that shit. I had the biggest fucking
bubble-snot crying session known to any one human being.
And I am for certain that I came within inches of busting
one of my tear ducts. I thought about all the memories me
and my mom shared. I was grateful for all those memories. I
was even more grateful for the last four months we shared.
After her diagnosis, we had bonded even more. I looked
at the old pictures of my mom that I had stolen from my
grandmother's house and I reminisced about her beauty.
I thought about the times when I was a little girl, and I'd

patiently sit on her favorite wooden footstool with my arms on my knees holding my head looking at her get ready for date night with my dad. I cried. Oh, I cried. And then I felt some more. Everything. I felt everything. I felt every single emotion that weekend, good or bad. Once I started to smile at some of my memories, I knew that was me honoring that detachment from my mom: not as a curse but as a life lesson.

Once I was able to get completely quiet in my head (read: meditation), I was able to understand the necessity in honoring my detachment. In both the relationships that I've treasured and the ones that have caused me burden over the years. This concept of detachment being a life lesson was needed in order for me to live a peaceful life. It was needed in order for me to move past my grief.

"It was my letting go that gave me a better hold."

—Chris Matakas, *author of*
#Human: Learning To Live In Modern Times

But that meant that some people weren't going to be able to sit at the winner's table with me. Even if they were my family. It meant that I wasn't going to allow them to treat me like shit just because they were family.

It meant that I had to cultivate a willingness to contently let go of some things and some people. That's what detachment is. Because we all live intensely codependent lives, detachment can feel like it's an act unworthy of our commitment. We allow our families, communities and our jobs to define

> *Detachment allows a certain type of peace...*

so much of us that oftentimes we are not even able to figure out what to do next. So much of their behavior influences our own. Detachment allows a certain type of peace that lets us truly love and embrace those people who've earned a spot on our journey with us. This process gives everyone the freedom to grow and find his or her own peace. While honoring the detachment of my relationship with my mom was the suckiest shit I've ever done, I had to do it. It was the ultimate price that I had to pay for her love.

When I wasn't embracing or honoring that detachment, I was miserably letting my ego play a game it could never win. My ego always wanted to ignore my feelings in an effort to try and control the outcome of the inevitable.

Ain't none of this shit promised or certain. Detachment taught me that I had to control my efforts, not the outcome.

{ When family won't let them go on in peace }

I don't think any of us were really ready for this kind of detachment. My whole family thought of ways to save my mom from dying. Because at some point, we all believe we are God, right? When my mom and her doctors decided that it was time to end her fight with cancer and go home with hospice, my dad vowed and almost threatened to take her to Cancer Treatment Centers Of America. I definitely found this idea to be laughable. She had been through five months of chemotherapy and radiation, and the cancer was aggressively spreading to every organ in her body. But he had watched countless testimonials of sick people who were miraculously not sick anymore after being treated there. I don't think I ever paid that much attention to those commercials. But my dad did, and he started to believe my mom's doctors were wrong about her death sentence. They had given my mom just a few weeks to live, and my dad thought the doctors had failed her and her family.

We never made it to Cancer Treatment Centers Of America.

I felt like I was the only person in our family that understood what hospice was. It basically meant that my mom was going to gradually die. And remember, the fact is death comes for all of us with certainty and it's inescapable. Eek, that sounds really awful. But I need to warn you and tell you the truth about hospice. Hospice means that your loved one will comfortably wilt away into nothingness until their last breath. All of their organs will eventually stop working, and they will die. The nurses will keep them as comfortable as possible, but the goal is not to keep them alive. That is the ugly, blunt truth of hospice.

We elected for in-home hospice. It felt like the most natural way to die. My mom had signed a DNR (Do Not Resuscitate) form, so it just made sense that she was at home for her last days of living. She'd still have access to a 24-hour hospice nurse, the social worker and home health aides would also still be available. Not only would it be more comfortable for my mom, but it would be more convenient for family and friends who wanted to come and spend time with her. It was a way that she could peacefully die. But the objective was still to die.

Since I was the only one who really knew how to use the Internet, I did a little research on what dying of cancer would do to your body—per my family's request. I tried really hard to educate them, but they were not ready to accept the truth, my mom's truth. I read that at some point she'd completely stop eating. I read that at some point her urine would turn to a rusty brown color. I read that at some point she might not be able to walk on her own. I read every single article I could find about how people die of cancer. I printed out everything I found on the Internet and put it in a community folder in our kitchen labeled "Things To Know About Mom's Cancer" for everyone to read at his or her convenience. No one read it. They refused to. And my mom got tired of saying no to people trying to get her to eat or drink. She'd do anything you'd want her to do if that meant you'd go away. That was our inside joke. "I'm just entertaining those fools, Ty. As if food is going to make this shit better," she whispered to me. She'd give me little side eyes whenever her sister tried to get her to eat. One time it was some fresh, hot and juicy Royal Farms fried chicken with potato wedges covered in hot sauce and ketchup. Now it was just becoming silly, so I went off!

66

...I just wanted my mom to go in peace.

99

Short of cursing out my mom's sister, I told her everything my mom wanted to say to her but was too polite to let out. "Just stop," I said. "This is ridiculous, don't you fucking people know that she has stage 4 lymphoma. She has cancer! She is going to die. Fuck! We are all going to die. If not today, maybe tomorrow, or maybe the next fucking day. But my mom is going to die!" Well, maybe I did curse her out a bit. Anyways. I let the words linger in the air a bit before I stomped off down the hallway and out the back door. Of course, I intentionally slammed the door as my aunt rushed behind me. I just realized that I haven't spoken to her since that day. I'm sure she's waiting for me to apologize. Well, if you're reading this book Aunt B, sorry!

But I just wanted my mom to go in peace. It was the least that we could do for her. We had all been hanging from both of her tits (my dad included) for most of her adult life. It was time to detach. I wanted her to be able to enjoy the family and friends that she loved while she still had a little time left. I wanted her to be able to be mean to all the annoying bastards (even if that meant being mean to her sister, too). She deserved that much. My mom had done what my dad asked her to do. She fought cancer. She fought cancer even though all she really wanted to do was to live out her days without the treatment. She fought cancer for him. And what did she get for fighting? She was still dying. I wanted her for once to think of herself first. I wanted her to have a little peace before she left us. Wasn't that the least we could do?

Having to let go is hard. It's hard to imagine your life without them. But that's selfish. And, I realized that I couldn't be selfish. I had to let my mom go in peace.

Living and Loving, Independently

Learn to live independently.

Don't let your family's past experiences…

define you.

They make only one chapter…

of your book.

Detach yourself from hatred disguised as love.

Realize that even your family

can be toxic to you.

Don't judge your family for their inability to love you.

Love them…

no matter

where they are

in their journey.

Chapter

03

The art of losing

{ Pain vs. Suffering. }

Somewhere around my mom's second round of chemotherapy, I learned the difference between pain and suffering. My grief has taught me that you can experience pain without having to experience suffering. Pain is inevitable. Suffering is optional. Pain is just a part of nature. Suffering is that pain married with constant resistance. I believe that if you are truly facing adversity and you're struggling to process your grief, you have to allow yourself to end the suffering. You have to be ok with the fact that you might always be in pain because of your loss. To always have pain in your life doesn't mean you are suffering, or that you have to suffer. Your acceptance does not equal approval. This was one of the very first lessons I learned after my mom died. Believe it or not, we all choose to experience every emotion we go through. We all choose to be happy. We all choose to be excited. We all choose to be fearful. We all choose to be mad. But pain is a feeling that happens as a result of something traumatic happening (and I use that word really loosely). Suffering is the emotional reaction we *choose* to let happen as a result of our pain.

"

Pain is inevitable.

"

"We turn pain into suffering by adding on all kinds of beliefs, interpretations and judgments to it."

—*Brenda Shoshanna, author of* The Zen Road to Happiness:
Simple Steps to Attaining Peace of Mind

The spoiled little girl in me would so love to tell you that you could stop the pain from ever infesting your life. I'd also like to tell you that those unicorns and fairies are real and not just fictitious characters in our bedtime lies that we tell our children. The truth is that pain is normal, and no matter how much you think you can shelter your heart, you will always experience some level of pain. It's part of being a human being. On a very basic level: when you fall, you hurt your leg. You feel pain. The next part of your journey should be learning how to repair the pain. But instead, we often throw suffering into the mix of our emotions. Suffering is all those icky layers we put on top of our pain for it to make sense to our brains. The "I can't believe this is happening to me, again." Or the "This kind of shit only ever happens to me." That, my beloveds, is suffering. It's the absurd commentary the voices in our heads recite to us frequently enough that we start to believe it's true. And because we're human, and feelings rule the world, we think that the "story" or the "suffering" is the most important part of the journey instead of owning the emotion and moving forward.

Watching my mom go through chemotherapy was beyond difficult because I knew that she was in a lot of pain. There were times she couldn't even see. The tumors had spread to above her eye, and she woke up one morning and she couldn't open it. And when she could see, everything tasted like what she called a "brand new shiny quarter" (read: when you have cancer things may start to taste like metal). During the last four months of her life, she wasn't eating anything at all but (and, this is graphic) she was still releasing decades worth of fluid that was still in her body. Yet, somehow she refused to suffer and managed to always smile through her pain.

She had been in the hospital for a few weeks, and I had to make sure that I warned the staff about my mom's "special" conditions. They weren't, like, really special, they were just all the things the CNAs usually forget or purposely look over because they are paid peanuts and fairy dust. Before I'd go home each night, I'd leave a note on her chart with every detail they needed to know. She hated jello. She wanted lots of ice chips, but no water (because she knew they weren't coming back for hours, so she'd let the ice melt). And the most important note that I highlighted and wrote in all caps was for the nurses: "IF YOU CAN'T GET THE IV IN, CALL HER DOCTOR." My mom's veins were so teeny-tiny that they often liked to play hide and seek with the nurse's needles. I made sure to explain that to everyone. That wasn't the cancer. It's just genetics, because my veins are just as disrespectful. And that disrespect makes it hard to put IVs in.

One day, I walked in on a frustrated, near irate nurse struggling with my mom's wrist. Be clear: I basically freaked all the way out. My mom, on the other hand, was not freaking out enough as far as I was concerned. And if she had planned on freaking out, it was taking her way too long to do it. "Let's give her arms a rest, you can come back a little later!" I said in the snappiest dismissive voice I could find deep down in my soul. But my mom, who was a part of the kind-folks crew, smiled through her pain and said, "it's ok, let's give it a try one more time!" That one more time turned into a messy, bloody failure and lots of redness on my mom's wrists. There was mucky blood all over her pillows I had just brought in from home, on the muted cream hospital sheets and in my mom's hair. We joked about it later that evening as I tried to tackle cleaning dried blood from her hair. Jokes and laugher were how my mom dealt with her pain. She wasn't a big fan of suffering.

> **"**
> *...I was all in my feelings again.*
> **"**

My mom was an "it is what it is" and "it's gonna be what it's gonna be" type of woman. And that's how she parented us. She just didn't understand complaining a la suffering. It was some years after Pebbles had died, and I was all in my feelings again. I had another kiddie panic attack, wishing I had my bird back again. I was hyperventilating while stomping up and down our hallway pouting and basically letting my thug tears win at life. My mom was in the middle of cleaning up, so I kind of knew I was in the way and bothering her Sunday routine. But I wanted my bird back. When I walked past her for the umpteenth time, she slammed the mop in the bucket of water and softly screamed, "Listen! The bird. Is gone. There's nothing you or I can do about it. Please! You just have to stop thinking about that bird and move on. Simple! You hear me?" When she got mad at me her words always shook me to the core. So I sadly nodded my head "yes" and moved on to playing with My Kid Sister doll because (1) I refused to willingly subject myself to beatings, and I knew that was the next step if I kept "trying her patience" and (2) she was right!

Suffering is like a form of self-induced torture that we allow our minds to endure. Not surprisingly, some of us do this on a daily basis. I could sit and think about how much I miss my mom and how we didn't get to spend more time together before she died. But I will always miss her. That is a fact that I cannot change. My mom was just fifty-eight when she died. She won't get to see me do so many things. She's missing what I think are my best years. She didn't get to see me get married, although I still ain't married (looks to my boyfriend for the answers!). She didn't see my son graduate from high school. She won't read my first book. There's so many "she won'ts" that I could focus on. And, honestly, I'm not perfect at this grieving shit, but you know why I can't let myself suffer? I've been so afraid that if I allow myself to suffer, to constantly think about the "she won'ts," then I won't be able to remember the great parts of our world. And, oh my God, we had so many great parts! There were our family movie nights. They were always epic to me, mainly because of the comedic relief my parents' love for movies and sleep offered up. Both of them would fall asleep and somehow magically wake up whenever me or my brother tried to change the channel. Damn! I wish that social media was around back then because that battle should have been captured and shared with the Internet. I think it would have gone viral. On special Saturdays (my mom declared which ones were special), we'd spend nearly an hour driving to have dinner in Delaware. Delaware was where the closest malls and restaurants were. And even though my dad dreaded the drive, that's where we'd spend our Saturdays whenever my mom asked to go out to dinner. My mom loved Red Lobster, and my dad loved my mom.

It's those memories that keep me from letting my pain transition into suffering. And because of that, suffering just isn't an option for me. And it shouldn't be for you, either. Suffering takes up valuable real estate that my memories have already claimed.

{ Don't let the guilt suffocate you }

But after I finally taught myself how to stop suffering, I still had work to do. I had to stop feeling guilty. I had to release myself from the burden of guilt that most mourners carry whenever someone they love dies. Every once in a while, I replay the last argument that my mom and I had. We fussed over who would cook the baked ziti for dinner, her or me? I know, I know, replaying this moment in my head is totally "suffering," and I said we shouldn't do this. But I promise you that all the things I tell you not to do (or to do) in this book are really just reminders for me.

"Guilt is perhaps the most painful companion to death."

—*Coco Chanel, fashion designer*

I am pretty sure that my mom secretly thought that I could not cook. Which is a fair, and kind of semi-accurate, assumption since she never really showed me how to cook (insert kiddie pout). I can do the basics of any Cooking

101 class. My mom not teaching me how to cook really wasn't her fault. She just couldn't. She adored doing things for us. Her goal was to spoil my dad, my brother and me. Family was her first priority. She always had to take care of her family, and cooking was one of her duties. So I grew up just *watching* my mom cook. But all I was ever able to do was cut the vegetables using her "As Seen On TV" cutting board thingie, boil and peel some eggs or hand her things out of our lazy Susan cabinet. Even though I wanted to help, she never let me. Because she was a control freak, and had to do things her way all the time, I was her little sous chef. Since all I ever did was watch her cook, I knew everything that there was to know about how my mom cooked. I was always amazed at how things tasted the same every single time even though she didn't use measuring cups or cookbooks. I've adopted her methods as an adult, and I know it's cooking by taste. She'd add a pinch of this or that, and if it didn't taste right to her (or me or my dad) she'd add some more of this or that. So I knew exactly how to cook all the things she cooked, like baked ziti.

We were a few weeks into her being home with hospice. I could tell that she was tired. She had tried cooking and cleaning the day before and failed. She was getting to the point where sitting up was almost a struggle for her. Cooking for her family was out of the question. I decided that I wanted to cook dinner for us. I was in the kitchen

cutting up the vegetables and cooking the ground
beef when she stormed in. Unlike her, I was a multi-tasker.
"What are you doing?" she screamed. I'm like: "Duh, mom,
I'm cooking."

66

...this would be the last argument
we'd ever have.

99

(But I'm still her child so this was just a thought. I dared not
to disrespect her, even in my thirties.) I mustered up a loose
version of a sweet and polite voice and said, "I'm making
us baked ziti for dinner." As my lips let go of that last word,
I instantly thought to myself: this will be an argument.
I tried to get a hold of it, like I'd do with most of our
mother/daughter spats. But this one was different. It almost
felt like my mom knew this would be the last argument
we'd ever have. So now I'm yelling, she's yelling. I'm
fighting back tears, she's still yelling. My voice starts to
tremble as I spit out my reasoning for why I can do this. I
feel like a dumb, overly emotional teenager. Like ma'am, it's
just baked ziti! But then she hits below the belt and pitifully
says, "I might not be here this time next year." It was like
she was performing her last show, and she just dropped the
mic and sashayed off the stage. That hurt my entire gut.
Her words snatched my soul from my body.

But as soon as she put the period on her sentence, my mom went back into the living room and laid down in her hospital bed almost like nothing had happened. Like she had won. Meanwhile, I fought off my thug tears with all the energy I had left inside. I was unsuccessful. I had a breakdown over the Cracker Barrel white cheddar cheese and organic noodles.

We had lots of arguments, but I replay this one in my head a lot because it represents how damaging my guilt can be to me. When guilt appears during grieving, it's a normal, yet unnecessary, emotional response. We have this perception that we've somehow failed in what we think are our duties or obligations to the person who has died. Yes, it was just baked ziti, but that argument represented every dispute we've ever had. And, now that she was dying, none of them were ever worth it.

She was right; this could have been our last argument (and it was), so I walked into the living room ready to apologize. It was the first time I really told her how much I loved her and that I didn't want her to die. I mean, I had just found my footing in my life and I was starting to create a space of my own in this world. And now she was leaving me and I had to figure this out all by myself. Aww, hell nah! I mean it was just last week that I had even decided to grow up (even though I was 36 years old). Adulting was really new to me, and I was eager to show my mom that I knew what I was doing. That I could do this by myself. My mom was going to miss so much of my new adult life. I also finally 'fessed up to what I think she already knew: there was a huge part of me that was livid, and resentful, that she waited so long to seek treatment. My mom knew that something was wrong, but she let fear invade her better judgment. She had been unusually tired and sick since the beginning of that year. She would always say that she just wasn't feeling right. How many of your loved ones have said that? I told her so many times to go to the doctor. I almost begged her. And, when she finally did, she had stage 4 lymphoma. I was so emotional. I blurted all that out, too. And then I wiped my tears from my face and ended our argument with a reminder of how salty I was because she lied to me about that "damn bird."

Looking back, I know that that part of the argument with my mom, that session of judgment-free conversation, was exactly what I needed to not feel that burden of guilt. In a time where she was at her most vulnerable, I was able to be completely transparent with her. And I believe that it meant just as much to her as it did to me.

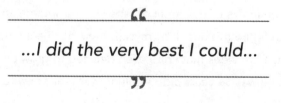

...I did the very best I could...

Just like you, I've had my share of "what ifs," "should haves" and "what if I had done a better job at fill-in-the-blank." Sometimes I wonder if I should have just let her cook that baked ziti. But the truth is: I did the very best I could under the circumstances. Even at my worst, it was all I had left to contribute to part of our journey. And I had to believe that or I'd torture myself with 20/20 hindsight, which we all know proves absolutely nothing. Unfortunately, we do a lot of that kind of thinking in the beginning of our grief. Take this advice as gold: if you can be truly honest with yourself and your loved one, then the "letting go" process won't last nearly as long.

{ What happens after you say goodbye }

When the doctors had tried both chemotherapy and radiation and nothing was working to kill off the cancer cells, my mom was forced to make a difficult decision. After she convinced my dad it was best for her, she was sent home with hospice. The doctors initially gave her two or three weeks tops to live. I tried to begin the letting go process mentally. I thought it would be easier for me if I just accepted the fact that she was dying. Why fight it, right? "It is what it is and it's gonna be what it's gonna be" as my mom would say. So I helped to write her living will. That first week home with her I wrote and proofread her obituary. And even though my mom was being cremated, my dad had to have a funeral. So I picked out something for my mom to wear at her wake. As her oldest child, I felt it was my responsibility to make sure everyone knew what my mom wanted in her last days and beyond.

I stopped praying for her to live...

But her last day didn't come in two or three weeks like her doctors had promised. She stayed home with hospice service for almost four months. I was beginning to think she really wasn't going to die and that this was all just one long ass theatrical episode of *Punk'd*. I stopped praying for her to live and I started praying for her to die because watching cancer torment her body was awful. Her skin was grey and felt like the inside of a worn suede shoe. It was weird to touch. Her beautiful grey hair had been replaced with dark brown scabs. She'd randomly beg for my dad to hold her because she was afraid to let go, but I think she knew that she needed to. Everything that physically made her my mom was gone. Watching her like that made my "letting go process" a cumbersome task to complete. I became detached. I was going through a serious identity crisis. One minute I was her loving daughter, who wished for nothing more than to have her live forever and always, and then in just seconds I'd become a complete stranger to that pain because I knew that dying this way was cruel and evil, and

I just wanted it to end. I was so emotionally charged and completely drained at the same time. When my mom finally died, I was cold and unbothered. I was relieved that the torture was over. But then I quickly realized…it was over.

Suddenly, I couldn't breathe! It was a fact (to me) that the world had tilted on its axis that April 28, 2013. Each day was the ultimate chore to complete. I'd open my eyes and just lay in bed for hours. Sometimes I'd simply wake up in tears. Some days I would just sit in silence unable to speak at all. Everything about my life was so hard to do without her. All of a sudden I needed her for everything. And then, of course, everything great that could possibly happen for me actually happened. I was on the *Today Show*. I was getting paid to travel and see the world. And then life served me with the most bittersweet cupcake: I was featured in all of these magazines for the grey hair that she taught me how to shamelessly love. My mom's hair was always envied by the women in the town that I grew up in. It was something out of an old black and white Hollywood flick. My mom was my first visualization of what beautiful was. I had always seen myself in her, and I secretly wanted to grow up to be her. I wanted her to know that I had finally arrived at the place she said that I would: that place of confidence and no fucks given that you arrive at once you get past a certain age. I was there, and I wanted to call to tell her. But I couldn't. Even though I was overwhelmingly comforted with Hallmark-inspired texts from family and friends and random emails signed off with sentimental quotes and scriptures from my blog readers, I felt completely alone. I wanted to scream and crumble to pieces.

"
I gave myself permission to forgive myself.

"

I screamed! I decided that in order to survive (and not suffer) I had to scream. God, I screamed so loud. I cried so hard. I had to give myself permission to scream, cry, pout and start that process all over again if I needed to every chance that I got. I had to give myself permission to madly miss her because I do. I had to give myself permission to feel unreasonably lonely without her because I do. I had to give myself permission to be utterly compassionate for myself because I am. I had spent the last six months of her life, our lives, being one of her caregivers. I was the only one who could get her to swallow all of her medicine without fussing at the world when her throat gave up on her. I made sure her little African print headscarves were on tight and straight whenever she had company at the house. I clipped and painted her unruly cancer nails while we watched the "stories" together even though she'd fall asleep in twenty minutes. I gave myself permission to forgive myself. I forgave myself for not letting her cook the very last baked ziti for her family. I forgave myself for all the lies I ever told her. I decided to take care of myself because my mom wasn't there anymore to do that.

I know we all grieve differently. My story isn't your story, but here's what I know to be true: we all have good days, not so good days, and some really fucking horrible ass days. Promise me you will do yourself a favor and give yourself permission to cry whenever you feel like you need to because that's how you say your goodbyes. Promise me you'll be okay with excusing yourself from those triggering situations (mine was the usage of the word "mom") because that's how you say your goodbyes. Whenever your grief is unbearable, realize that this time is yours. So turn your phone off, decline those heart-to-hearts and love yourself like you know your loved one would want you to.

Grieving on Your Own Terms

Realize that, when you are caring for the terminally ill...

...what you give at any moment is 100% the best you have in you.

Don't let the guilt suffocate you.

Politely decline the love you can't handle from your friends and family.

Grieve...

...on your own terms.

Pain is a built-in feature.

There's no escaping it...

... So don't curate your life's story around the setbacks.

Instead, intentionally tell a story of unruly happiness.

Chapter

04

The how
of grieving

{ Good grief: What are the five stages of grief and how long do they last }

"Grief never ends... But it changes. It's a passage, not a place to stay. Grief is not a sign of weakness, nor a lack of faith... It's the price of love."

—Unknown

When you first experience death, especially the loss of a parent, there's a void. That void was what I woke up to every morning after my mother died. It's the last thing I felt before I went to sleep. It's something that I am conscious of all throughout my day when I stop doing things to distract me from thinking about the void. That void is perfectly explained in the research done by Swiss psychiatrist Elizabeth Kübler-Ross. I've experienced *every single one* of these emotions nearly ten times over and in no particular order.

Denial.
Anger.
Bargaining.
Depression.
Acceptance.

Denial. This emotion was something that didn't immediately surface for me. I even feel a little guilty writing this, but I knew my mother was going to die. It had become a reality for me. There are some parts of this journey that I just forget. I don't really remember the funeral. I just remember not wanting to be there. My mom was being cremated. I thought the whole ordeal of having a funeral just for family's sake was dumb, so I pouted my way through it after I recited my poem. And that's all I can remember.

But I remember the summer of 2012 like it happened this morning. It was the middle of July and I had come home to Maryland to visit. Mainly to get my first taste of my mother's infamous crab cakes. This was a summer tradition for me. I was a little worried before I got there. My dad had already told me that she hadn't eaten more than a few saltines in the past thirty days, which I knew to be odd because she loved cooking for us just as much as she loved eating with us. But she always worked way too hard, and too long, so I just figured that maybe she needed some rest. When I got home, despite not feeling too good, my mom was still able to slay all day over a hot and buttery cast iron skillet for my crab cakes. So I was hoping it was just a thing that would pass.

It was just a few days later when she was diagnosed with stage 4 lymphoma. The devastation in the doctor's voice the day he predicted my mother's fate was deafening. It felt and sounded hopeless. I could see the doctor talking, but I couldn't hear anything. His words were paralyzing but filled with power. There was nothing about that moment that led me to believe she was going to make it through this battle with cancer. So you see, I had been prepping my mind and heart from the moment the doctor said, "Can you excuse us, I need to talk to your mother in private?"

...Cancer is stealing my mom...

But denial hit my dad quickly, and heavily. I remember riding in the car with him coming back from one of her hospital visits. It was maybe three weeks into my truth of "Cancer is stealing my mom and I fucking hate life!" He said, "I'ma save my girlfriend." He called her that sometimes. It was one of the many things I loved about their relationship. After my dad got clean, they were in love again. Growing up it was nice to see. It made me believe in love in a way others knew nothing about. And my dad was proud of that love. As I was talking about her chemotherapy treatments I brought up some alternatives, he stopped me before I could finish talking and said, "You just don't understand, Ty. Because you'll never love your mother the way I do!" I stopped listening.

Pause!

Fuck. My feelings were hurt. They are hurt! They still hurt
to this very day. It was a declaration that cut the insides of
my heart into tiny pieces and left me wondering how he
could ever think my love for mom was inferior to his. But
I guess the truth was, he'd known her longer. Truth was,
his love *was* stronger. Truth was, his love *was* first. And I
guess because of this superior love that he believed in, he
just couldn't let go. His love has kept him in denial, and
subsequently I am still waiting for my apology.

For me, denial showed its true colors on my first birthday
without my mom. Like each birthday, I was too excited to
get to hear from my mom. It was our traditional, annual
phone call that really never lasted more than ten minutes.
But I always knew it would end with my mom saying, "I
love you" and "See you soon." I remember waiting for
hours. Near the end of the day I was almost in tears, mad
as fuck wondering why my mom hadn't called me yet. It
was maybe 4 o'clock in the afternoon when my phone
rang. It was my son calling to wish me a happy birthday.
My son dealt with my mom dying just like I did, quiet and
to himself. I wanted to hug my son and crowd his heart
with hugs and kisses. He said he promised to call me every
birthday, just like mom-mom did. My heart sank to my toes.
I realized, again, that my mom had died and she wasn't
calling me ever again.

Those moments that I forget she's gone happen often enough that they fuck my entire head up. It's those moments that cause my denial to be the catalyst for my anger.

Anger. From the moment the doctor said, "Can you excuse us, I need to talk to your mother in private?" I started to question why this had to happen to *me*! To *our family*. To *my mom*! Hadn't we been through enough already? I was barely "unbitter" from my dad's stint in the rehab facility when I was a kid, I was only two seconds from not being jealous of the attention my brother got from having sickle cell and now when I am finally making something of myself as a writer, God decides it's my mom's time to have a seat in the Upper Room. I finally have something for her to be proud of and she's not here. I mean shit, there are tons of neglectful, horrible mothers out in this world. Why did God have to take my mom? It all just made no sense to me.

―――――――――――― **"** ――――――――――――

Please excuse me, my mother just died...

―――――――――――― **"** ――――――――――――

The first year without my mother I had a disclaimer. That disclaimer was for everyone I knew, everyone I came in contact with. My co-workers, my boyfriend, even strangers on the street. And it was simple. Whenever my emotions were triggered and I wanted the grieving process to be over I'd say, "Please excuse me, my mother just died and I am angry as fuck!"

I still find myself angry on some nights. After my day is done and something great has happened, I just wanna tell her. Even on the days were nothing really happens, all I ever really want to do is hear her voice again. I miss her voice the most. When she first died, I would call my parents' house just so that I could hear my mom's voice on the answering machine. Then I'd hang up. My dad eventually disconnected their phone service because who has landlines in 2016, right? There went that torturous obsession. Not being able to talk to her makes me angry sometimes. A lot of times, actually. I didn't visit home as often as I should have, but talking on the phone was our thing. My mom and I would talk on the phone for hours. Well, she'd talk and I'd listen. Every couple of minutes, I'd throw in a word or two so that she'd know that I was still there and still listening. My mom loved to call me to talk about her day. She'd talk about all the crazy things that happened around the house. She'd talk about what she ate and what new recipes she found to tweak. Sometimes she'd just call to recap the "stories." She knew that I didn't watch, but it didn't matter to her. She just wanted to talk. I deeply miss those phone calls. And sometimes missing her this much makes me mad.

"
...I really begged God...
"

Bargaining. When my doctors and my mother decided that it would be best not to fight the cancer anymore, I immediately got on a bus from New York to Baltimore. At the time I didn't completely understand what hospice was, so when my mom told me that's where she was going I thought maybe she was dying in a few hours. That was the first time I really begged God for something. It was the first time I really prayed for something and really wanted it. I mean, I had prayed to make the cheerleading squad and I prayed that God would have the baby delivery people come back and get my little brother, but none of that was important. Now, I was asking for a real problem to be solved.

I prayed to God and asked if I could have my mom here with me just a little longer. Christmas came. My dad put all of our decorations up just like she would have. My mom was still here. Since God answered my prayers that time, I tried again right after the holidays. I prayed the hardest that evening. I closed my eyes really tight and put on my best "I'm a Christian and even though I don't go to church please help me God" voice. I asked God if I could have her just a little longer, maybe until her birthday in January. Her birthday came. We celebrated with balloons and some cake that she couldn't taste because cancer sucks. But she was still here. So I sent up *another* prayer asking if I could keep her until my son graduated from high school. Maybe God knew I was being greedy and was over me begging. She died that April. Bargaining was over.

Depression. Man, listen. Depression, well, it comes and goes and goes and comes. I first admitted that to myself when Karyn Washington committed suicide. She was twenty-two. Karyn was a popular beauty blogger from Baltimore, Maryland. She advocated for the acceptance of dark skinned women. I instantly felt a connection to her because I had spent my adult years in Baltimore, and Karyn's first email to me landed in my inbox about four months after my mother had passed. Like my mom, her mother was losing the battle to cancer. And Karyn was now prepping her next moments of life without her rock. I gave her some tips. Like: make sure you take pictures of you and her holding hands. Oh, and record her voice for later (one of my regrets!). We exchanged emails for the rest of 2013. I re-read her emails over and over again with the intention of checking back on her, but I never did. My own grief got the best of me, and I completely muted myself from our conversation. I'd occasionally see her blog posts travel down my timeline, but she never followed up so neither did I.

One day, I was indulging in my morning ritual: a deep scrolling through Facebook. After I skipped past a few status updates, I noticed a familiar name: Karyn Washington. But this Facebook post wasn't from her. It read, "Karyn Washington, founder of the blog *For Brown Girls* and popular campaign *#DarkGirlsRedLip*, has committed suicide." I paused and immediately hopped up out of the bed. I grabbed my laptop. Maybe my phone was wrong! This could not be true. Searching for the answers, or hopefully the lies, I clicked around Facebook. I went to Karyn's Facebook profile and instantly broke out into tears. Her friends and family had already begun to leave their goodbyes and messages of sorrow. I cried harder. I was speechless

I think that was the day I realized that I was depressed, and I couldn't hide it anymore. So I wrote about it on my blog. I confessed that Karyn Washington could have been me. I still think about her a lot. I never got a chance to meet Karyn. But she impacted me in such a way that I couldn't lie about my depression anymore. I remember how much of a wreck I was that morning. I taunted my depression, and I read each goodbye message her friends left on her Facebook page. There were thousands of them. Then I taunted my depression a little more and read the emails that we exchanged over and over again. I often think about what more I could have said or done for her. I should have called her. I should have asked to visit with her. I could have saved her, I thought.

Before accepting death, we unwillingly discover guilt. You know, because we didn't do enough. We didn't say enough. We didn't feel enough. But the truth is, I couldn't save Karyn Washington anymore than I could have saved my mom. And that was the beginning of my depression. It comes and goes and goes and comes.

Acceptance. I had left my Brooklyn box to be by my mom's side back in Maryland. I stayed with her up until the last two weeks of her life. We did regular girl shit. Shit me and my mom never did on the regular as mother and daughter before she got sick. Her nails were growing out of control, so I gave her a manicure, painted them this obnoxiously bright Tiffany blue color. I somehow convinced her against jet black. She begged me to watch *Sparkle* with her. And I did. Five times. The morphine just wouldn't let her be great, so she ended up falling asleep every time. She just would not give up on finishing the movie. So I watched it five more times while she fell asleep.

I was on their couch, and I woke up one morning feeling so empty inside. I had lost myself somewhere. This experience was slowly and quietly killing me. Each day was spent watching her body melt into nothingness. My main task was to help her swallow the thousands of pills that she took only to make her comfortable. Everything I knew to be normal had been abruptly taken from me. I was fighting the process my mom knew as death...Apollo Creed style!

I had enough. Death was happening whether I was there by my mom's side or not. I had accepted that there was nothing I could do to save her. I decided to leave my parents' home and head back to New York. I told my mom early on that I couldn't and didn't want to be there for "the end." I didn't want my last memory of her to be her taking her last breath. I never wanted to know what that looked like. So I told my mom that I loved her and that I would be back in a few weeks. When she was first sent home for hospice the doctor said it would just be a few days or weeks. It had been three very long months, and I was starting to think we were being *Punk'd.* Two weeks later, my dad and my grandmother held my mom's hands as she took her last breath while I was in New York...trying to live my life. The guilt that I had to accept, my darlings, is *so* real!

Our brains are so much smarter than our hearts. It's normally the one that reminds me I can't call my mom to tell her that this imposter syndrome got me all the way fucked up in the game. I'd have to explain to her exactly what that meant, but that was the joy of our thing. Our relationship. I've learned that acceptance doesn't mean that I'm happy again or not depressed. It just meant I'm not foolish enough to dial my mom's number and expect for her to answer. It was moving past the depression.

Now I embrace immortality because, like I said, we've all been duped...everyone dies. But what no one tells you is that these stages of grief never fucking end. You grieve for fucking ever. It's your new fucking normal. I can't tell you how many times I repeated these steps wishing and hoping I was done only to exhaust one emotion and move on to the next one.

Denial.
Anger.
Bargaining.
Depression.
Acceptance.

REPEAT.

These stages revolve in and out of my life like my high school boyfriends. And they break my heart just the same. Thanks, Elizabeth!

{ When the loss sinks in: Coping with grief and understanding your "new normal" }

About a year into processing my grief, I found myself sitting naked on the toilet, boohooing my eyes out on the phone to my best friend, Anitra. She's my person. When the world has completely stopped giving fucks about my dreams and goals, I call her. So that morning when I woke up distraught and ready to end my life, I called her in a full-on bubble-snot cry because I couldn't stop full-on bubble-snot crying. I didn't give her my normal, "Gurl, let me tell you what happened today!" greeting. It was just a frantic, skipping voice followed by sniffles and obscure words that even I couldn't understand. I didn't know what I wanted to say. But I was waiting for her to stop me. She didn't say anything for about fifteen minutes. She was just breathing. We were breathing together. She was breathing heavy enough for me to hear her. Heavy enough for the sound of her breath to cue my brain to cue my heart to stop that emptiness feeling that was causing my tear ducts to bubble-snot cry. And, eventually, they did.

This, my beloveds, is my "new normal."

I know this shit sucks!

My mother going to the Upper Room (because I believe Heaven is where all great human beings live after death) changed me. It made me vulnerable on purpose, yet at the same time I became this bonafide grown ass woman who suddenly needed to make decisions on her own. The matriarch of our family was gone. I no longer had this woman who loved me and cheered for me regardless of how immensely ambitious my ideas were. Now matter how dumb my idea may have been, she was there rooting for me. I now had to root for myself. This, my beloveds, is my "new normal."

Nothing about life for me could or would be the same after my mother died. Carrying on with my life as normal would only be more harmful, and it would be an injustice to our great relationship. I kept thinking, "So I'm just supposed to move on with my life as if I haven't lost the greatest love I've ever experienced." That's not how any of this works, people. This was...the price of love! This, my beloveds, is my "new normal."

That Monday after she left me for her spot in the Upper Room, I knew that what I had been thinking all along was true. Angels and unicorns and baby Jesus really do exist.

All the people that came by the house to be nosey and look at her dead body had left. The coroner came and took her body away earlier that day. The night came, and while my dad, my son and my brother had all managed to fall asleep, I was on the couch bubble-snot crying. I looked out into the sky through the window. I immediately paused my session of tears. The moon shined so bright that night. I couldn't sleep, so I just stared at the moon for hours. I stared at the moon until it wasn't there anymore. When my head finally got heavy and I was forced to close my eyes, I saw her. I couldn't believe it. My dream was in color. She sat with me and we talked for what felt like decades that night. We even went shopping for a bit. When I finally woke up I was in tears because (1) it felt so fucking real and (2) I wanted so desperately to go back to sleep so that I could see her once more. Just to be sure, I walked out in my parents' living room to say good morning to her. I was hoping this was all some terrifying nightmare, only to find her empty perfectly made up hospital bed. This, my beloveds, is my "new normal."

I find myself counseling other women who have lost their mothers, and there's always one common thread between us: this "new normal." Once I understood that this new normal had to exist in order for me to survive and *not* want to take my own life, or someone else's for that matter, I felt like I had conquered my grief. Kinda.

Effectively coping with your grief means that you will need to surrender all of yourself to your emotions. And in order for you to surrender, you must first acknowledge that those emotions are there. Then, you must feel them. If you are like me, acknowledging your feelings might be like forcefully stepping into quicksand.

> **...suffocating your feelings only suffocates you**

And once you step in this quicksand (voluntarily) you get to this place where you willingly allow short, ugly, strong trolls dressed in sequins to repeatedly beat on your heart. No one wants to go through that bullshit. But suffocating your feelings only suffocates you. So I learned how to cope with my mother's death by finding three things...gratitude, purpose and faith.

Somewhere after I buried my mom, the way I thought about life and death changed for me. I realized that God couldn't possibly hate my mom, or my family, or me. He wouldn't have us travel down this incredibly, almost insanely, difficult path without some kind of purpose, right? So in order for me *not* to flip all the way over and out from watching my mom's body deteriorate into eighty pounds of nothingness, I had to figure out how to have gratitude in my journey.

First, I realized how many people never get to have a relationship with their parents, especially their moms. And here I've been blessed with this super-fulfilling relationship with my mom. When I looked back on my life and thought about the woman I'd become, it was all my mom's doing. From how I spoke to people, to how I styled my hair and let it turn grey, even to how I perceived my own beauty. That was all my mom. It's because of our conversations, from birth to death, that I am who I am today.

I used to sit patiently on a footstool in my mom's bedroom. I'd sit with my arms holding up my head and I'd gaze at her reflection in the mirror. My mom represented my first visualization of what beauty was. I was so fascinated with watching her interact with people. She was my fashion icon. I was a kid when someone asked me, "Little girl, what do you wanna be when you grow up?" I said, "Denny Brown!" I wanted to be her when I grew up. I studied everything my mom did. When she talked with my dad she'd playfully twirl her long, signature ponytail. It's a habit that I subconsciously picked up as an adult. So you see I can't waste any time thinking about how different my life is now. I'd die if all my spectacular memories of my mother and me left because I wasted them on grief. Somewhere along this journey I started to become just grateful, ya know. I was just grateful to have had a mom like mine in my life. I was also grateful that my mom wasn't suddenly snatched from my life.

I got to spend every day of her last year present on this Earth reminding her of how much I loved her. I learned that, as bad as it may seem, I am grateful to have had her in my life for thirty some years.

Before my mom died, I think I spent what seemed like all of my life searching for my purpose. My biggest question was: what do I want to do with the rest of my life? On my list of what I wanted to be when I grew up were: a teacher, a nail technician, an actress. Of course, being Denny Brown was at the top of that list. I realized that I was thinking way too hard about this "when I grow up" question. My purpose was so simple! I have this need to inspire and impact people to live. Whether it's to inspire you to quit your job and move to New York, or finally head back to get your master's degree, or maybe it's just as simple as going to your first Broadway play—my job is to stimulate you to make a change in your life to live!

Lastly, there is faith. It only takes a mustard seed of it, right?! As a not-so-faithful Baptist church-goer, I do remember reading the Bible, which mentions faith a lot. As a little girl, I had no clue of what that scripture meant or what a mustard seed was. When I realized my mom was going to die, I remember asking my social media family for their prayers. I thought that if everyone who was on social media (which is everyone in the world) prayed for my mom, then she'd be cured of cancer. My relationship with God was…distant at best. So I figured if I asked everyone and they all actually prayed for my mom that God couldn't ignore that. She got sicker!

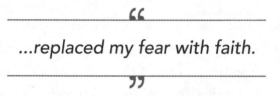

…replaced my fear with faith.

My mom confided in me one night at the hospital. She said she had faith that this was the right thing. She wasn't scared at all. In the beginning, I did it for her. Because she asked. I replaced my fear with faith. I began to notice that wasn't a one-time action, and it wasn't just because my mom asked me to. I wasn't just saying: "I got faith" and hoping to be blessed abundantly. I actually believed that one day I'd be ok with my mom's death. That one day I'd no longer be scared of living without her. I had faith I'd see and feel this day eventually.

This, my beloveds, is my "new normal."

{ Things no one wants to hear or see when they are grieving }

The one thing I know for sure is that every day in the beginning of grief will absolutely suck. Birthdays and holidays were the hardest. The Internet is the main culprit. It makes the process of grieving really unbearable at times. On Mother's Day at every corner of the Internet you can find a mother and daughter duo posted up enjoying hugs and kisses followed by overly sappy verbiage from Hallmark. Cue thug tears!

When it's not a birthday or a holiday, your friends, family and strangers will have no clue what to say after you unload the dreaded statement: "My mother passed away..." And, it does not matter if you say it happened last week or twenty years ago, America's universal response will always be: "I'm sorry to hear that!" This must be taught in college, right?! It's a constant funnel of *I'm so sorry your life now fucking sucks without your mom* (the dramatic kid in me comes out sometimes).

And maybe you can tell that story about how your best friend's cousin's sister's daughter also suddenly died from cancer, but now is probably not a good time. Grieving shouldn't feel like some sort of heartache competition.

But I do get what you're *trying* to do. You think your storytelling time will give a valuable and relatable perspective to my feelings. But here's what ends up happening instead: It really just starts to sound like the death of my loved one doesn't count at all. And I am pretty sure that's not what you meant, right?

Even I stopped saying: "I know exactly how you feel," because actually, I don't. Yes, I too lost my mom to her rightful place in the Upper Room, but I don't really know how you feel. Relationships are not cut-and-dried. They are personal. They are exclusive. So my relationship with my mom wasn't the same as the relationship she had with my brother or my father or my son. So actually, I don't know exactly how you feel. And while, yes, we've all been majorly duped because death will happen to us all, telling someone you know exactly how they feel makes it seem as if their loss is somehow routine and ordinary.

Let me also tell you what else my mom's death was not: a blessing in disguise. I can't tell you how many times I heard this after my mom's long and debilitating illness. If death is the relief from that long and debilitating illness, then it's not a blessing. My mom truly suffered from cancer. On the Thanksgiving before she died, I woke up to her panicking and weeping for help like a baby. Her eye had completely shut close. The visual I have from that evening still haunts me. We learned that another tumor (by this time there were tumors in her liver and pancreas) had formed above her eye. I watched my mother fight like Rocky for the next eight months only to have cancer eventually eat away at her body. Death was a relief for me, but never a blessing.

I often get a little cynical when someone who is, say, ninety dies. You think: well they lived a good life, hopefully! They've seen a good number of their friends find their rightful place in the Upper Room years prior. Maybe it was just *their time*. But now I know that my thoughts on grieving for the old are a bit naive, and it's easy to start to take our elderly for granted. They've been a big part of our lives for so long that we start to think they will be with us forever. They've lived through the illnesses, the falls in the bathroom, and the unexpected operations, but they still beat the clock. They somehow now seem indestructible to us. Until they are gone. And while we've all been duped about this whole death thing, we should believe in death but not take our grief for granted. It will knock you on knees whether your loved one is two or ninety-two.

> ## ...in reality no one really wants to die.

I was having a conversation with a few friends. One of them has recently lost their brother at war. He was twenty-five.

Our friend said, "At least he died doing what he loved, serving our country." Nope! And I'm sure you can hear the silence of that day, too. None of us knew exactly what to say in response to that bullshit. The reason why I keep reminding you that we've all been duped about death is because no one talks about it. No one says: "Well if I gotta die, I'd wanna die doing this or that." Because in reality no one really *wants* to die. You can stop saying this, too.

So let me help you out. Because there are a few really cute and simple ways to console us (me in particular), and I find them all to be really comforting. I love when a stranger says, "Aww" and their eyebrows kinda frown a bit. It looks like that sad face one teary-eyed emoji. That's a perfectly good response. If you have to follow that with an I'm sorry to ease your comfort level, go for it. After all, this is all about your emotions not mine (read: heavy sarcasm). If you know me or you knew my mom, then I love hearing, "I miss your mom, too. Oh my God, remember that time…" Reminiscing about my mom with other people makes it feel like she's still here. Her memory never dies. And it also reminds me that I'm not entirely alone in this.

I know you guys mean well when you say things to comfort our grief, but often hearing no words at all is sometimes better comfort than hearing the wrong words.

Your New Normal

Surrender…

…to all of your emotions

…So that you can breathe again.

The thug tears, the kiddie panic attacks, the outbursts of anger…

They're all part of your new normal.

Don't fight it.

Grief is now a part of you.

Death makes everyone…

…uncomfortable.

If you're not the one going through the loss…

…then remember it's about the mourner's comfort

and not yours.

Chapter

05

How to be obsessively grateful

I think a lot of us assume that being grateful will be second nature, but that's definitely not the truth. Especially when you try marrying the idea of being thankful for the things you have in your life with the void left by someone you've loved beyond words. Lord! It will almost always take a back seat in your everyday life. Being grateful is something you have to constantly practice doing and work really hard to be good at.

In 2013, I began what I call the most "awake" years of my life. If you were to ask anyone, I had it all. My life was enviable. I was living a dream life. I was living a life most people would kill for. I still do little happy dances and pinch myself at the opportunities that I get to experience. I still don't talk to my dad that much, and he has no idea what I do for a living. Whenever we do talk he's guaranteed to ask me, "What do you do again?" He just knows that people pay me to do some really cool shit and I'm able to pay my overpriced New York rent because of it.

But after my mom died, I started to notice that I could barely see or feel any of that joy I had created for myself. I was officially on autopilot. My mother was dead and so was the only family I'd ever known. She was the glue that held it all together for us. I would only ever call home to check on her. But whenever I called home, she'd make sure to find my brother and my dad so that I could chat with them for a few minutes, too. My mom isn't here to make sure that we all talk. She's not here to make sure we're still a family. And I felt alone. Now that she was gone, it felt like I was standing on the emptiest emotional road ever. I felt cold and abandoned. The worst part was that I was all by myself holding shattered pieces of me. I was desperately trying to put my foundation back together. I had to finally admit to myself that my entire floor was just gone. Grief had slowly crept its way inside my heart, and it was blindsiding me with huge karate kicks to my chest. The pain of losing my mother had grown so rich with rage and hate that I didn't know who I was anymore.

I did what my mother would have told me to do had she been here to answer all the questions I now had. I became grateful for all the things I still had in my life.

I remember as a kid I would complain about our dinner options. I could almost bet what my mom would be cooking for dinner each day of the week. The rotation didn't change much, if at all: meatloaf, spaghetti, baked chicken, pork chops, fried chicken and maybe on Fridays we'd get treated to a trip to Pizza Hut. Or Chinese food. Redundant much? Being the emotionally-charged, spoiled kid that I was, I'd fuss and pout because…meatloaf! I still hate meatloaf to this day. "Ugh, meatloaf again. We had meatloaf last Tuesday and the Tuesday before that. When are we gonna have something different?" would be my opening statement before I sat down at the dinner table. She would normally just ignore me. She knew I was a fat kid at heart and I'd eat just about any and everything she placed on my favorite She-Ra plate (because I am a real 80's baby!). But after my 432,904,171st outburst of dislike, she decided that she had had enough of my mini tantrums and said, "You gonna eat that meatloaf and whatever else I put on your little plate. Be grateful that you have food to eat every day." Of course she dropped the mic with this; "There are people in Africa who are starving." At the time, all I knew was those infomercials of starving kids (I guess they lived in Africa, who knows?) and that made me feel super bad about not wanting my food. I stopped complaining.

My mom would remind me how important it was to be grateful as many times as she felt I needed to hear that lesson. It was an unconscious effort for her. My mom was one of the most gracious people I've known, even during her chemotherapy. When that tumor had swollen her eye completely shut, I was panicking. But she put her hand over mine and sweetly said, "Well, damn, at least I can still see out of my other eye." We both laughed a bit. Inside my heart cried droplets of thug tears, but I still got her message. I remember when her hair first started to fall out. I offered to just cut it off for her. I figured it would be easier for her to accept losing all of her gorgeous hair.

Because that's what I would do. But she said no and wanted it to fall out on its own. She said she wanted to experience all that cancer had for her. Even in all that she had been through, the chemotherapy, the radiation, the surgeries, she was able to be grateful for the moments she was still able to experience. No matter how hard that experience was. I admired that. I remembered that. I knew I had to duplicate that idea of thinking in order to survive my grief.

"Your greatest joy is your sorrow unmasked."

—*Kahlil Gibran, author of* The Prophet

Being grateful means that each day we seek satisfaction in the simplest things. It means that we view every little twinkle of life as a blessing. I call them the "but I woke up today" moments. The "I was only two minutes late for work and I didn't get fired today" kinda moments. It's so clichéd to say, but there really is someone out there who's worse off than you. And there's someone else worse off than them. And then there's someone else worse off than them. The cliché lives a thousand lives and moves in a trillion circles because it's the truth. I had almost four months to really prepare for my mother's death. While I promise you that it was the most difficult thing I've ever been through, I often wonder what my life would be like if she had been unexpectedly snatched from my world. What if I never got to shape and paint my mom's cancer nails? What if I never got to watch *Sparkle* with her a trillion times while she fell asleep? The devastation would still be just as real for me, but when I looked at things in retrospect this is why gratitude is important in grief.

"

...gratitude is independent of your life circumstances.

"

First, know that gratitude is independent of your life circumstances. I realized this when I decided to move to New York to pursue my career in writing not even a month after my mom was diagnosed. Even though I had already given my resignation to my job and secured my uncomfortable couch in Harlem, I had not told my parents yet. I was waiting for the perfect, foolproof moment to tell them that I was leaving my good government job and my beautiful third floor downtown-ish Baltimore apartment to become an editorial assistant and sleep on someone else's uncomfortable couch. It didn't seem like an idea that my parents would get behind. Plus, I hadn't quite figured out how to package that up to make it sound like the incredible idea I knew it to be. I also faced an enormous amount of guilt. Now that cancer was dominating most of our daily family conversations, I was debating on whether or not I should just ditch my crazy big dreams and stay in Maryland to help take care of my mom instead.

We were alone in her hospital room one night. My dad left to look after my mom's patients. Her passion had always been to care for others. She took care of both my great-grandparents until they died because she hated the concept of a nursing home. She thought that it was so impersonal and dispassionate. She believed that nursing homes could not give the elderly or the mentally disabled the care that they deserved. So after I graduated high school, she quit her job at the local meat factory and started a home healthcare business. My parents bought a huge house that rested on about six acres of land and she created an assisted living facility right inside of our house. I was so proud of her. She's the real reason I'm an entrepreneur today. We all pitched in to help her. Sometimes I'd miss out on a party or two because I was helping my mom do things with her patients. But I loved helping her. Ms. Melvina, Mr. Larry, Mr. Frank...they were her patients but they had become our family, too.

My mom made sure none of that changed when cancer arrived. During her chemo treatments, my dad and I would take turns keeping my mom company or staying at home to take care of my mom's patients. That night I was flipping through the channels and I discovered some balls and just said it: "I'm moving to New York." Surprisingly, the parent rant of how crazy my dream was that I had expected never happened. Instead, she asked me if this was what I really wanted to do and whose uncomfortable couch would I be on. She held my hand and tearfully congratulated me. She said she'd support me to the moon if that was where I wanted to go. She said she was just grateful to have such a talented daughter like me. A daughter that wasn't afraid to go after her dreams. She said that she admired me for that. I thought: Me?! Lord, let me tell y'all that the thug tears skeet-skeeted down my face so fast. I couldn't believe that during the most vulnerable and challenging time of my mom's life she was still able to be grateful for me beyond her own circumstances.

But if you think about it, it's really hard to think about your own shortcomings when you are grateful for someone or something else. It's hard to focus on all the negative points in your life when you are overwhelmed with gratitude for what you have. Being grateful for my journey, for the fact that I had a mother who was always without a doubt present in my life, for my new career—that got me through my darkest days and essentially saved my life. There were times where I didn't want to live anymore. Like I said, I could have been Karyn Washington. There was a time when I just couldn't see my life without my mom. But I was able to re-center my life through gratitude. I no longer felt as unsatisfied or as lost without my mom because now I was focusing on all the great things I had received from our relationship. All the great things that I still had in my life. I couldn't see it in the beginning, but being grateful changed how I grieved.

{ How to discover the power of your words to manage your grief }

The real question for me then became: how can I constantly live inside these moments of gratitude? And was that even possible for me to do? Especially after losing my mom and now dealing with the tremendous anxiety of not knowing what was next for me. I had just moved to this big city where I knew no one. I was working at a new job. I was experiencing these new things without my life support— my mom. Living inside moments of gratitude meant that I had to be ok with whatever my life handed to me. And, if and when I finally figured out how to be ok with that shit, I couldn't talk myself out of being ok with that shit.

Because of my blog, I had arrived at this place of "celebritism." Most bloggers get to this faux-celebrity life because they have tons of Instagram followers and swoon-worthy website traffic. But thanks to the Internet, I was famous because I shared my story about my mom. And now a lot of people, a lot of you, could relate to me. I was bombarded with sympathy cards and well wishes from complete strangers. It was overwhelming for me. I found myself answering five or six emails a week from women who had lost their mothers and were seeking guidance. From me?! But the problem was that I had curated this life on the Internet that wasn't real life for me. People thought I had this grieving thing all figured out. This book will make you believe I have this grieving thing all figured out. But when I was alone with my thoughts, the "every day is gonna be a bad fucking day because my mom is dead" thoughts, I realized that what I said to myself, both out loud and subconsciously, mattered. I could see that the words and advice I shared with my readers had become this vehicle for expressing and sharing my experiences with them. And that changed how they experienced their grief. But what I didn't realize was that the words I was habitually choosing to use with myself were affecting my personal experience.

> **"The tragedy of life is what dies inside a man while he lives."**
> ——*Albert Schweitzer, philosopher*

I have a friend who is huge on the belief that what you speak out loud will manifest in your life. She's the friend who can recite *The Secret* and makes you create vision boards with her every three months of your life. She'll even help you frame them. I swear we all need her in our lives. She suggested that I do some research on transformational vocabulary. It's the idea that if you change the words you consistently use to describe your feelings and emotions,

> ## ...*every word you speak has the power to build or destroy...*

then you can change your perspective on the life you're living and truly create the life you want. Think of it as your verbal vision board. It's the difference between saying that you're "scared to death" about changing your career path or admitting that you are just "feeling a bit uneasy" about it. It's the difference between saying that you're "really livid" that he canceled your date with such short notice or admitting that you were just "slightly disappointed" about it. The bottom line is that every word you speak has the power to build or destroy your hopes and dreams. Your words can slowly mend the feeling of loss or cause those feelings to magnify into a million pint-sized slow deaths that eat away at your soul. Everything we say, or think, has the potential to either heal us or harm us.

Once I realized that my self-talk was absolutely sucking the entire life out of me, I had some real work to do. I went back to work directly after my mom's funeral. Bad fucking idea. I should have gone on a solo vacation or something. I constantly led my days with my emotions, so I was always late for work. I didn't care. I couldn't focus, so I was handing in piss-poor assignments. I didn't care. I had started to lash out at my co-workers and, guess what, I didn't care about that, either. My feelings mattered over everyone else's. Everyone needed to care about how I felt *first*. My daily disclaimer would be, "My mom just died, I get a pass." At the time this seemed normal because…grief! But it was just an unhealthy way of thinking and acting. I was so filled with depression that I was dying on the inside, and I had to change. I wanted to change.

I started writing down short, positive affirmations in the mornings. I posted them all over my office desk and randomly wrote them in my personal journals. I wanted to be able to see them unexpectedly. I would compliment myself in the mornings before I left out for the day. I'd say to myself, aww I look mad cute in this dress. Or shit, this dress makes my butt look really big…in a really good way. Then I made a list of positive power words. That's deep, right? I know! It's one of the best ideas I ever googled. After doing some research on how to use them, I knew that the more positive words I collected for my vocabulary, the more likely I could communicate my emotions with clarity. Using positive power words made sure that I wasn't leading every conversation I had with, "My mom just died, I get a pass." I learned the true power of my words when I started responding to people rather than reacting to people. Please trust that learning to become non-reactive is a continual challenge for me. In a conversation the difference between reacting and responding to someone is about five to ten seconds of thought. But once I was armed with my positive power words, I was able to respond in a way that colored my true feelings. I was no longer held hostage by the chaos of my emotions. I had created a routine where I was able to speak great things into my life through my words and my thoughts.

{ How to create routines for healthy grieving and finding strength in unexpected places }

Everything that could possibly change in my life changed once my mom died. The hardest part of my grief is accepting the unending absence of her. Death. Is. Final. She is never coming back. Even the things or people that I thought I could count on felt very different to me. I tried to enjoy the holidays and birthdays without her, but it was and sometimes is torture. My first Christmas without my mom was utterly painful. She adored Christmas. I think it might have been her favorite holiday. Like, her adoration brought out the most obnoxious decorations imaginable. Everything was gold and big...and gold. She had an emerald green tree that almost reached to the top of her ceiling that somehow she managed to decorate the same exact way year after year. It was like Disney magic to me. It almost looked like one of those pre-decorated trees you get from Target. Of course, I could never help my mom decorate because it had to be done *her* way. So I ended up just handing her the ornaments along the way. Even though as an adult I hadn't been around in years to actually see or faux-help her put the tree up, I resented the fact that the option to help was now gone. But I had a choice when it came to how I adjusted my life to accommodate my grief. I could pout and have kiddie panic attacks at each holiday and birthday or I could create new traditions and routines for my new normal.

So instead of wallowing in my holiday grief that first year without my mom, I decided to spend the holidays with the Broadways. The Broadways are some of my family members from my dad's side that live in Delaware. It's my dad's sister and her daughters and their daughters. Growing up, I didn't spend much time with them because we were always hanging with my mom's side of the family. I feel like I missed out on a lot of memories with them. I barely know my dad's side of the family. But as an adult I had become really close with my Aunt Katy. When my mom died, Aunt Katy promised her she'd take care of us. She's probably the only family I really talk to. You could say she's my favorite aunt. What's even more hilarious and endearing about that is my aunt will tell you, without pause, that I am her favorite niece. It's her greeting whenever I walk into her house. My aunt has been so instrumental in my grieving process by allowing me to create new routines around her immediate family. She knew that I needed to be reminded that there was love still present in my life. When we're grieving sometimes we forget that. My aunt knew that I needed to be loved.

"

...living and loving others was the ultimate way to honor my mom's love.

"

When we're grieving sometimes we forget that, too. She was there in the beginning to help me pick up all those broken pieces left from the void of my mom. And sure, she can't put that fixture of love that my mom and I shared back together again, but it was nice to have someone help me carry those broken pieces. My aunt showed me that living and loving others was the ultimate way to honor my mom's love.

After that holiday, I noticed how much happier I was. I'm not perfect, so I'll admit to you that sometimes I still let my sad head spaces get to me. But creating new and unexpected traditions and routines allowed me to work through my grief in a safe and constructive way. So I wanted, and needed, more routines. I wanted to perfect how I experienced my new routines, my new normal. I had a blast that Christmas watching my little cousins open their presents in front of family, but it was still so hard to watch. Seeing them enjoy the holiday with their mom made me miss my mom even more. So now each Christmas my boyfriend and I go away for the holidays. I loved those moments with my aunt and her family, but I needed to experience the holiday in a new way. In my own new way. This year my boyfriend and I are taking a twelve-day cruise with his family. Pray for ya girl!

"

...my new routines always save me...

"

Believe me, we all wish we weren't members of this club where Facebook's "On This Day" memories bring you to tears, where you have sweet dreams of your loved ones only to wake up and realize that the nightmare of loss really happened, where each deathiversary feels like the very first one. Your loved one is gone, nothing is going to be the same and you need to acknowledge it. Accept it. That's what I repeat to myself, daily, hourly, sometimes every few minutes. I think I've written that in some form or another at least five times in this book. But it's a truth that no one tells us. And that's why my new routines always save me from breaking down at every mention of the word "mom." You can passively assume that through the years everything will work itself out, but I'm telling you that's a lie. You have to consciously and repeatedly create routines that remind you how to love and live again. Or your grief will become unbearable.

> **"I never travel without my diary.**
> **One should always have something**
> **sensational to read on the train."**
>
> —*Oscar Wilde, playwright*

I've always kept a journal. I had a purple diary with silver glittery hearts all over it that my dad always broke into and read. He thought he was slick. He really thought he was doing something, too. But I kept my real secrets in an old composition notebook labeled "Math Homework." I left it out on my stereo, and he was none the wiser. As a writer, keeping a journal has always been my practice. Right now at my desk I have about eight empty journals just waiting for my words. Now, I journal for about twenty minutes a day, and when I am too busy to write a few paragraphs I use the fill-in-the-blank method.

Today I felt sad when...*I thought about calling my mother. I miss her voice the most.*
I am thankful for...*my boyfriend's shoulder. I don't know where my tears would land if I didn't have his shoulder.*
3 things I did well today...*I did my makeup in less than ten minutes. I was on time for work today. I walked five miles.*
I am thankful because...*I was able to walk five miles without my knees giving out on me.*

I found that journaling helped manage my grief in my own personal way. It was my self-care. My journal became my all-accepting, non-judgmental friend who listened attentively every single time. And isn't that why we pay for therapy? We just want someone to listen us, without interruption and without judgment. In real life, I could spend a grip on therapy and I've thought about it...a lot. But after a year of journaling my feelings about my mom's death, I looked back and my read words and I saw my progress. Journaling provided me the cheapest therapy I've ever had. I was amazed at how far I had come since the first words I had written.

August 16, 2013.

I just can't shake this feeling. This feeling of guilt and sadness. Sometimes it overwhelms me. I don't want to leave this bed. But when I do, I try to keep busy. Someone suggested that I keep busy. Never stop moving. That helps me ignore the fact that she is gone. But like for real for real, she's fucking gone! And still it doesn't even seem real to me. My mom is dead! I tried to call her last week. I finally figured out how to make the perfect homemade crab cakes. I was so excited to tell her that I totally forgot she had died. The pain is becoming overwhelming. Sometimes I just want to die. It cripples me on most of my days. I lay in my bed just staring at my ceiling until almost two o'clock in the afternoon. All I can think of is my mom. The things we did together. The things we haven't done together. I had this dream that we spent all day together, shopping and talking and more shopping because anyone who knew my mom knew she loved shopping. My dream seemed so real though. I remember in my dream I was taking a nap and my foot was hanging off the bed a little. I swear I felt my mom touching my foot. I woke up and jumped out of the bed hoping I could catch her before she left but it wasn't long before I figured out that I was just dreaming. I spent the rest of the day crying...

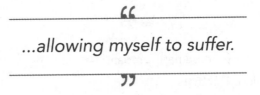

...allowing myself to suffer.

That's the first paragraph of my first journal entry after my mom died. When I read that now, I remember how much pain I was in. I can see how much pain I was allowing myself to be in every day. I was allowing myself to suffer. I was swimming non-stop laps in that shit. I am still so surprised that I am here. Sane. I am surprised that I'm even able to write and talk about my mom without the tears. And, of course, I still miss her in a way that I cannot describe, but I'm not crippled by my grief anymore. I've created enough routines, journaling being the golden gift to myself that teaches me how to live an abundant life again. I no longer want to die.

These routines have offered clarity for my thoughts and my feelings. I've gotten to know myself better. I know without a doubt what things make me happy and what things make me feel confident about living well again. I also realized what things were toxic for me. I want to be happy and celebrate life.

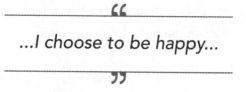

...I choose to be happy...

Now I choose to be happy regardless of the experience I am having. That's gratitude.

Your Clarity, Your Purpose

Everyone isn't blessed…

…with the greatest love of all time.

So be grateful that you are one of the lucky ones to have received it.

If you can manifest…

a new belief, that is centered on you being ok,

then you will be!

Routines will offer clarity and give purpose to the unwanted new normalcy of your life.

Chapter

06

Things every mother should tell her daughter

Looking back now, I know that my mom and I had a legendary kind of relationship. From that damn bird to our very last goodbye, she was my conscience, my cheerleader, my protector…she was everything that I didn't know I needed until I needed it.

I was in middle school when I met this boy that I thought I was going to marry. Y'all, he was so fine. We met at a church dance. We did the slow grind to Bobby Brown and Babyface for what felt like hours, and I fell head over heels in love. I mean I was almost a stalker for this boy. Damn shame I can't even remember what his name was. Let's call him Aiden (even though his name was probably Devonte or something). I've always loved the name Aiden. But it didn't take long for Aiden to convince me that I was almost a grown up and my mom was being way too strict with me. I lived a pretty sheltered life. No boys. No lip gloss. No parties. And definitely no boys. He lived about an hour away from us, and no matter how many times I asked my mom she refused to let me go and see him. So all we could ever do was talk and giggle on the phone late at night. Oh and there was also absolutely no talking to boys on the phone, so I'd sneak on the phone after my mom went to sleep. Mind you, I was twelve and he was fifteen. Girl!

Aiden eventually put the idea in my head that I should run away from home. He thought it was so ridiculous how my mom was treating me. I couldn't do anything but go to school and come back home. So one night during our giggle session he offered to let me stay with him and his aunt. So I packed a small book bag full of essentials— my hair brush, my journal and one pair of underwear. I attempted to make my way to Aiden's house on foot and wished for a ride up the road. I didn't get very far before *everyone* in our town knew that I had run away. I ended up laying low in my great-grandparent's basement because they were way too old to even realize I was down there. I camped out, hungry as fuck, until they went to sleep around 7p.m. and then I finally found a way into their house to call Aiden. Do y'all know that ninja didn't answer any of my phone calls? I don't know if he changed his mind, or if his aunt said, "Oh, hell no." I never spoke to him again. God, I was angry. I felt like I had been humiliated by the love of my life. I wanted to die, but I had no idea how to die. So I reluctantly decided to go back home. Cause I wasn't fittin' to be homeless, I was too cute for that.

I was already heading back to my house when the cop that lived down the street from us found me walking on the side of the road. I was terrified. But not of the police. I remember telling the cop to just lock me up because the beating I had waiting for me would surely kill me. My parents both came to the police to station to get me. But I will never forget my mom's face. I'll never forget how sad she looked. I could tell that she was fighting back tears because she'd never let anyone see her cry. I had expected her to yank me up or choke me out when we locked eyes. But when she saw me she dropped to her knees and prayed.

"

I didn't need to run from her love.

"

We drove home in silence. Actually, it was silent around our house for a few days. Finally, my mom called me into her bedroom about a week later. She apologized. I was like: wow really?! I was so confused. But she said she never wanted me to feel like I couldn't be me. But I was an twelve-year-old little girl, and it was her job to protect me. She said she'd do her best to protect me for as long as she lived. She said that she'd be there for me, no matter the hour, wherever I needed her to be, and that I didn't need to run from her love. Then we talked about boys and those "birds and bees" that I got grossed out about. All I ever wanted to do was just sit and giggle with Aiden in person. I ain't want no parts of no birds or no bees.

"You can't be your best by yourself."

—Jovian Zayne, *professional development coach*

> ## ...*no one would love and protect me like my mom did.*

But through it all, my mom kept her promise. I always knew that no one would love and protect me like my mom did. That moment when I ran away and we reconnected proved to be more powerful than I could have ever imagined. It taught us both the value of transparency and the value of respect for people as both adults and children. Of course, my mom and I had lots of squabbles, and I may have bubble-snot cried throughout most of my teen years, but I still understood what her love meant to me. I never ever had to question it.

That's your job as her mother.

I've always believed that being a mother to a daughter is the sweetest and most complex gift that you'll ever receive in your life. You'll have a high level of responsibility with all of your children because you want to set them up for success. But being a mom to a daughter brings on a huge task. It's your job to help her become a woman. She'll grow up in a world that tells girls and women that they are not enough, and that will be challenging for you both. You'll want your daughter to be tough enough to score that CEO position at the top firm in the country but still be soft and pink enough for everyone to love her when she gets there. You'll want her to be strong-willed but still kind-hearted and gentle. At times, you'll feel like you're not good enough to be her mother. But you are. That's why God picked you as her personal angel both on Earth and in the life beyond this one. So you have to make sure she has all she needs to face the world without you.

> ## Start by telling your daughter that you love her.

Start by telling your daughter that you love her. Often. Tell her that her smile will be enough to wow the boys on any day. Her worth is not determined by her body. And while she'll have this innate desire to feel liked and accepted, tell her she has permission to fall in love with herself despite what others think of her. People will naturally love her when she loves herself. Help her hear her inner voice. It will help her feel confident enough to make her own decision without the influence of others, including you!

Tell her that she is worthy of a magical kind of love, and that she should run fast from anyone who doesn't believe that to be a fact. Those people have not earned a place in her life.

Tell your daughter it's important to treat people with kindness because you never know what others may have been through. Plus, mean girls never win. Peer pressure is a bitch, so you have to tell her that bullying is what cowards do, and that you're not raising cowards. Tell her it's ok to stand up for herself, for what she believes in, and for other people.

66

...life is far too precious to waste...

99

Tell her for heaven's sake that it's just hair. Seriously. She'll want it to be thicker or thinner or longer or shorter. She'll want to curl it or straighten it or color it or shave it. Let her do it all! Whenever she wants. Remind her that life is far too precious to waste so much time on the pursuit of a good hair day.

Tell her that it's so cool to be smart, and no one will ever be able to take that away from her. There will be a small window of her life where she thinks being smart is for dorks and no man will ever marry her. Remind her that she doesn't have to hide her brains for anyone, especially for "Mr. Right!"

> ## ...I promise you she's listening

When your daughter is heartbroken, she will need you the most. Nothing teaches a woman more about herself than her first breakup. So give her all the unsolicited advice you want. Even if she pouts and has little kiddie panic attacks, I promise you she's listening. Tell her that people are human and they will let you down. Her values do not belong to the world, and the world will always fall short.

Remind her that it's ok to have feelings. Give her permission to own her feelings and ignore the judgment that may follow for doing so. Remind her that feeling the pain of each one of her circumstances will prevent the suffering.

Remind her that people deserve second chances; no one is perfect, including her.

> ## My mom's death made me different.

"Believing you are enough means remembering that nothing in you needs to change to be loved."

—*Jess Weiner, author of* Life Doesn't Begin Five Pounds From Now

My mom's death made me different. It made me different in a way that I almost can't explain to you. It's such a bittersweet experience. But I know I am the woman I am today because of her love then and because of the love that was still there after she was gone. I still have moments, almost daily, where I can't believe my mom is gone. But I thank her so much for preparing me for this moment. It took me some time to see the lessons because I was left feeling alone and broken to the core. I never thought I'd be ok. And some days I'm not ok. But I'm managing better than most because of some of the things my mom taught me before she died.

So to every daughter and every mother out there, I challenge you to love hard. I challenge you to squeeze each other tighter and tighter with each hug. I challenge you to live every day in the faith of your love so that when it's not physically there you won't ever feel alone.

The Truth About Love

Never

        let your daughter

               leave the house

        without telling her how much you love her.

Be transparent

      and

          always tell your daughter

                  the truth.

Teach your daughter

      that she

          has to believe in her truths,

               even if you don't.

Chapter

07

Dear Mommy

"Even the darkest night will end and the sun will rise."

—*Victor Hugo, French novelist and poet*

I n the beginning, I was really ashamed to admit how depressed I was. I was ashamed to admit that I had thought about suicide. I was ashamed to admit that I actually wondered how much easier my life would be not to wake up every day in tears. I wondered what Mommy was doing without me. And although I've never had suicidal ideation (read: actually plotted my death), I still wondered what would happen if I just wasn't here. If life just stopped.

But each time my mind drifted to that dark side, I realized that at the core of my soul I am really a punk. I don't have the courage it takes to pull the trigger or swallow the pills. So instead I opened one of my many blank journals and started writing letters to my mom. Sometimes it does make me sad to know that she'll never read any of them. But something, maybe it's faith or hope, allows me to believe that my mom knows exactly how I feel. And maybe the letters aren't really for her anyway.

Yea. These letters are for my own sanity. For when I can't move. For those days that me and 3 a.m. are the best of buddies. For when my thug tears paralyze me. I wrote my first letter to my mom on the eve of her funeral.

Dear Mommy,

When I was six, you helped me find my own style. You'd make sure my hair was always neatly twisted with matching bow ties and barrettes. Every outfit I wore had to have a theme. Sometimes, I was a sailor girl. Sometimes, I was dressed like Jane Fonda with a bright red, white and blue headband, a colorful track jacket, and fluffy leg warmers. That look might have been my favorite. Oh, remember you used to dress me up like a glazed, porcelain doll with lace gloves and white stockings? God, I truly hated that look. But you made sure that even my play clothes were frilly and froufrou.

When I was thirteen, you taught me not to steal. By then, I loved being a girl and wanted desperately to be a woman just like you. I had found the perfect, fiery red lip—problem was, it was in your makeup bag. But I built up the nerve to take it, because that's what new teenagers do. I wore it for picture day, do you remember? Of course you never told to me that red lipstick would stain your lips. Needless to say, I got caught and was on punishment for a few weeks. That was the last beating I got, I think?! But I just wanted to look like you.

When I was eighteen, you taught me how to be a mother. We changed messy diapers together, and took turns *getting up at four in the morning to warm up bottles. But when I wasn't paying attention one morning, my son took his diaper off and smeared poop all over his crib. We laughed about that later in life. But back then, you taught me that he was my responsibility and that was my mess to clean up.*

When I was twenty-five, you taught me that I was great. Every idea I had was fabulous in your eyes. First, I wanted to be a nail technician, you said, "Go for it!" Then, I wanted to be a cartoonist, you said, "Well...you can draw really good, maybe you should try that!" Then I said I want to be a runway model like Naomi Campbell you said, "You can be anything, all you have to do is decide, babygirl!" I finally became a writer. And when I found my newspaper clippings in your scrapbook bag, I knew that you were proud of me.

When I was thirty-five and thought there was nothing else for me to learn from you, you taught me how to tackle problems with grace and elegance. I watched cancer take over your body and steal your gorgeous grey tresses but still...you smiled through every moment of that journey. Even when you were in pain, you held my hand and said that you would be ok.

The Monday after you left me, you taught me that angels were real. The moon shined so bright that evening. I couldn't sleep, so I just stared at it for hours. When my head got heavy, I finally closed my eyes and to my surprise you were right there. In dreams, you sat with me and we talked for a while. You knew that I needed that. I think you knew I needed to feel you once more. I woke up in tears because it felt so real. I walked out into the living room, only to find an empty bed.

It's true, your body will forever be gone, but I know that you're always here with me. In my dreams, through the voices of others, and even in how I look. When people ask me if I am ok, I promise to think about all the things I've learned from you and say: "I will be."

Please know that you are missed.

Forever your babygirl,
Ty

I read this letter at her funeral. Then I posted these words on my blog for the world to read. It was my declaration to my family, to the world watching, and to my mom that I'd be ok. It was a public service announcement to myself. I've been writing love letters to my mom ever since.

It's been three years since my mom went to Heaven. Somehow, I've found my own comforting rhythm. It's a beat that soothes my yearning to end it all.

People tell me all the time: "You're so strong!" God knows that is so far from the truth. I am weak. Daily. I am vulnerable. Daily. And I know that's what's gotten me through all of my tragedies. I don't judge myself for bursting into tears in the middle of a meeting. I don't judge myself for eating the entire pint of butter pecan ice cream. I don't judge myself for being sad about losing one of the greatest loves of my life. I don't judge myself for being human.

I allow myself to pout for a few minutes. Sometimes I bubble-snot cry for hours. During times like these, I ignore the world's glaring eyes. Who says I have to be strong? Why do we all have to be strong?

We don't!

Unfortunately, grief doesn't come with an expiration date. The journey through grief is long and can feel like a never-ending experience. But remember that what you are going through is natural, and you are not alone. We all feel it. We grieve relationships. We grieve jobs. Hell, sometimes I grieve the last spoonful of butter pecan ice cream. But seriously, let grief run its course. Your faith will be tested. You will be weak. But that is what makes you strong, beloved. Be vulnerable with yourself, your friends and your family, and you'll be able to find the beat that keeps you from ending it all.

Acknowledgments

Finishing my first book was nothing short of a collaborative process. I thank God for surrounding me with fearless cheerleaders, devoted prayer warriors and audacious champions of healing. Truly, there aren't enough words to express how much I appreciate you for helping me achieve my biggest life goal. So let me just say thank you.

Thank you to my mother for showing me a love that's so great it shall never be equaled. Your spirit, your smile and your words will always be the core of who I am. Your wisdom and love will never be forgotten.

I thank my family—especially my favorite Aunt Katy and my cousin Carla. You guys have shown me how to love again in a time when I didn't realize that I had forgotten how.

To the love of my life—Mike, you've been my biggest cheerleader and loved me even at my worst. I am still in awe of the evolution of our love. I hope you know that I'll love you beyond my time in this world. Cheers to the next twenty years!

To my son—Khari, you are my greatest accomplishment. You are brilliant and smart and handsome. The world is waiting on your greatness.

To my PLP (Platonic Life Partner), aka my best friend, there are endless imaginary hugs and kisses for you whenever you need them. Anitra, your dedication to your growth and the growth of others motivates me to be better.

Thank you to my new family at Mango Publishing. I can now call myself an author thanks to you guys. Thank you for all of the hour-long Skype calls, the follow-up emails that I ignored and the pep talks you gave me when I didn't think I'd ever finish this.

Thank you to my all digital soul sisters: Christen Rochon, Kela Walker, Danielle Young, Shamika Sanders, Danielle Gray, Christina Brown, Jessica Andrews, Tia Williams, Diana Ramsey, Shaina Harrison, Chante Burkett, Lisa Brown-Hall, Brandi Proctor, Keiona Siler, Sheri Booker, Marie Denee, Maui Bigelow…your continued praise and encouragement is magical.

Last but not least, to anyone I failed to mention: Please forgive me and know I am grateful that you have been with me over the course of the years.

About the Author

Ty Alexander is an award-winning New York-based freelance writer and editor who pens her musings on beauty, fashion, pop culture, health, and technology. Her powerful words, undeniable beauty and lifestyle savvy led her to her roles as HelloBeautiful.com's Style and Beauty Editor and the Editorial Director of Beautiful Texture's TalkingTexture.com. Ty has since moved on to build her personal brand, Gorgeous In Grey, from a personal blog to an online lifestyle destination with over 100K page views per month. Her dedication to beauty and authentic living have helped garner that impressive following and have even caught the eyes of Redbook Magazine, Huffington Post, Hype Hair, ESSENCE, CNN Living, NY Daily News and more. Labeled a "Top Blogger" by EBONY Magazine and Black Enterprise, it's clear that Ty's talents are unlimited.